Martin Luther's Travel Guide

500 Years of the Ninety-Five Theses

On the Trail of the Reformation
in Germany

Cornelia Dömer

New York and Berlin, 2016

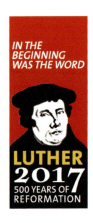

Martin Luther's Travel Guide
500 Years of the 95 Theses:
On the Trail of the Reformation
in Germany

Author: Cornelia Dömer
Preface: Professor Robert Kolb
Translator: Cindy Opitz
Editor: Eva C. Schweitzer

Cover Picture:
Wittenberg Market Square / Schweitzer
Luther: Lucas Cranach the Elder
Montage. Schweitzer

© 2016 Berlinica Publishing LLC
255 West 43rd Street, New York, NY, 10036
www.berlinica.com

Printed in the EU

Print book ISBN:
978-1-935902-44-7
E-book ISBN:
978-1-935902-45-4, 978-1-935902-46-1
LCCN: 2016954773

All rights reserved under International and Pan-American Copyright Law. No part of this book may be used or reproduced in any manner whatsoever without written permission except in the case of brief quotations.

Contents

Timeline of Luther's Life 5

PREFACE
MARTIN LUTHER TODAY 8
The Reformer and his Heritage
By Robert Kolb

INTRODUCTION
LUTHERLAND 11
Easy Travel from America and Great Britain

Luther Year 2017: Special Events 16

CHAPTER I
LUTHER'S UPRISING 19
Ninety-Five Theses and the Pope:
How the Reformation began

CHAPTER II
LUTHER'S TOWN 29
Lutherstadt Wittenberg,
Birthplace of the Reformation

CHAPTER III
LUTHER'S ALLIES 51
The Wittenberg Community
KATHARINA VON BORA 51
LUTHER'S CHILDREN 53
PHILIPP MELANCHTHON 54
ANDREAS BODENSTEIN VON KARLSTADT 55
GEORG SPALATIN 56
JOHANN VON STAUPITZ 56
JOHANNES BUGENHAGEN 57
FREDERICK THE WISE 58
JOHN FREDERICK I THE MAGNANIMOUS 59
LUCAS CRANACH THE ELDER 60

CHAPTER IV
LUTHER'S ROOTS 65
Growing up in Mansfeld:
A Tough Life Among Miners
BIRTH AND DEATH IN EISLEBEN 71
SCHOOL IN MAGDEBURG 79

Luther Trail in Saxony-Anhalt 87

Chapter V
LUTHER'S BIBLE 93
From the Wartburg to Weimar:
Traces in Thuringia
A PRISON IN THE WARTBURG 94
AN EARLY HOME IN EISENACH 103
AS A MONK IN ERFURT 109
LIGHTNING IN STOTTERNHEIM 119
GOTHA'S GARDENS 125
SMALCALD ARTICLES 129
SHOWDOWN IN JENA 135
WEIMAR'S CASTLE 137

CHAPTER VI
LUTHER'S MISSION 143
Spreading the Gospel:
Cities of the Reformation
LEIPZIG, CITY OF DISPUTE 143
HÄNDELTOWN HALLE 153
THE NAUMBURG CATHEDRAL 159
OUR LADY OF DRESDEN 161
TORGAU AT THE ELBE 165
LUTHER IN WORMS 170
THE REFORMATION IN SPEYER 171

Literature and Credits 172

Luther's Life: A Timelime

1483, Nov.	Luther is born and baptized in Eisleben.
1484	Luther's Family moves to Mansfeld.
1488	Luther attends Latin school in Mansfeld.
1497	Luther attends school in Magdeburg.
1497	Philipp Melanchthon is born in Bretten.
1498	Luther moves to Eisenach. He attends the parish school of St. George.
1501–1505	Luther enrolls at the University of Erfurt and earns the Master of Arts degree.
1505	Awakening experience in Stotternheim. Augustinian Monastery in Erfurt.
1507	Theological studies in Erfurt.
1510	Luther begins teaching in Wittenberg.
1510	Luther travels to Rome on a pilgrimage.
1511	Luther returns to Wittenberg to stay.
1512–13	PhD, followed by "tower experience."
1517	Posting of the 95 Theses in Wittenberg.
1518	Luther is summoned to Rome; speaks at the Diet of Augsburg.
1519	Melanchthon becomes professor in Wittenberg.
1519	Election of Charles V, Leipzig Disputation.
1520	Proceeding of Excommunication begins.
1521	Luther speaks at the Imperial Diet of Worms.
1522	Excommunication, abduction to Wartburg Castle; translation of the Bible into German.
1523	Luther returns to Wittenberg.
1525	Brings the Reformation to numerous cities.
1525, June	Marriage to Katharina von Bora.
1524	Diet of Speyer postpones the Worms Verdict.
1534	Publication of the entire Bible in German.
1536–37	Assembly in Schmalkalden; Smalcald Articles.
1544	Consecration of first Lutheran church in Torgau.
1546, Feb.	Luther dies in Eisleben. Smalcald War in July.
1552, Dec.	Katharina von Bora dies in Torgau.
1560, April	Philipp Melanchthon dies in Wittenberg.

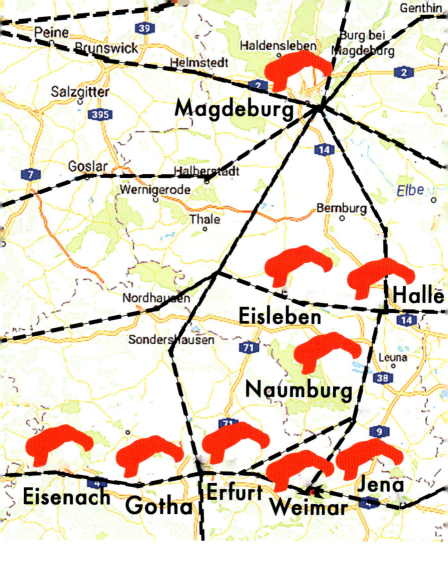

These are the cities in today's states of Thuringia, Saxony, and Saxony-Anhalt where Martin Luther lived and traveled. At the center is Wittenberg, where Luther was a professor and posted his Ninety-five Theses to the Castle Church door. He was born, raised, and died in Eisleben near Mansfeld. In Magdeburg, he went to school. In Eisenach, he visited the Theological Seminary as a student. Later, he was abducted to nearby Wartburg Castle, where he translated the Bible from Latin into German.

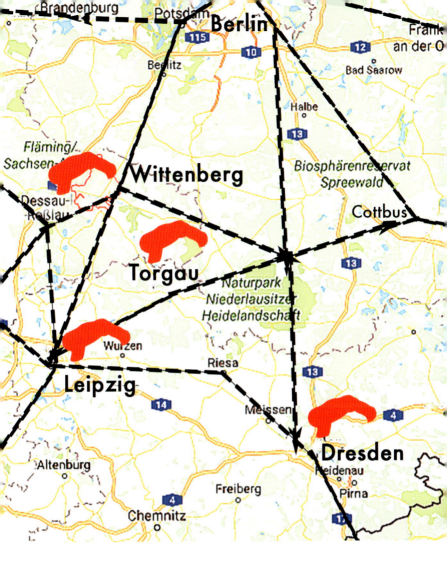

In Erfurt, he studied and joined a monastery. The Disputation with Johannes Eck took place in Leipzig. Important cities where he preached or consecrated churches are also indicated: Weimar, Gotha, Jena, Schmalkalden, Halle, Naumburg, and Dresden. His life-long mentor Frederick the Wise lived in Torgau, and Luther's wife, Katharina von Bora, was buried there.

The yellow lines are Autobahns, the black lines are railways. A trip from Eisenach to Dresden would take about four hours.

Preface

Martin Luther Today
The Reformer and his Heritage
By Robert Kolb

As the 500th anniversary of the initial events of the Reformation draws near, many eyes are looking toward the locations in which Martin Luther lived, thought, and worked. Although the Reformation had many facets and many antecedents, what happened when his call for reform found the medium of print in late 1517 coalesced personalities, public opinion, theological debate, political and social powers, into a movement with many aspects. What proceeded from Luther posting theses on indulgences at the end of October 1517 changed his world and shaped significant elements even of ours in the early 21st century.

God anchored human life in the soil from which he drew us. Our lives unfold in specific places, in the context of physical surroundings as well as a community of human beings. Our understanding of other people is enriched by knowing where they come from. Their geographical surroundings play a role in forming their intellectual and spiritual profiles as well as the political, social, and economic contexts in which they grew up and lived out their careers.

This volume is both for tourists who wish to visit the places of the Reformation and for those who do not leave their own homes far from Luther's German homeland. It enables readers who will never see Martin Luther's native turf to imagine more precisely how his life unfolded in the surroundings in which God called him to serve his church. It also provides a most helpful preparation for those who want to travel to "Lutherland" and see the sites themselves. It is the tourist's vademecum, to be thumbed while one walks through the streets and reviewed evenings after or before trodding in the Reformer's footsteps.

The author leads us through landmarks of Luther's life, from the ancestral home in Möhra to his birthplace, Eisleben, and Mansfeld, where he grew up, Eisenach and Erfurt, where he gained his education, and of course, Wittenberg, along with many other spots. Dömer accompanies us to the cities where he got his education, to the lonely spot where he decided to become a monk, and especially to Wittenberg, where small town life and the activities of a young university made their imprint on him even as he made his on them. With glimpses of other towns that played a longer or shorter role in his story, this volume leads readers through the events of his career. Dömer's effective recounting of the events of Luther's biography sets the framework for viewing the visuals that make this book unique. Attractive photographs and

Statue of Martin Luther, the German Reformer who translated the Bible into German, at Market Square in Lutherstadt Wittenberg. 2017 will be the 500th anniversay of Luther's Ninety-five Theses.

clearly laid-out maps of these places stimulate the imagination and afford a useful orientation for learning more about the Reformer's life and truly understanding this particular human being through a better idea of the particular surroundings in which he lived. The tools are here for guiding the reader's imagination into Luther's world.

Such a volume cannot include every place Luther visited. Despite being declared an outlaw by the German emperor, he traveled in his later years, for instance, to Leipzig and Torgau, to Marburg and Schmalkalden. In 1529, he journeyed to Marburg, where visitors can still see the table at which he sat with his supporter-turned-antagonist, Ulrich Zwingli. They disagreed over the presence of Christ in the Lord's Supper. Luther insisted that God conveys the Gospel to sinners through the bread and wine which deliver Christ's body and blood truly, in a mysterious manner; through the Sacrament, God continues to deliver "for you" forgiveness of sins, life, and salvation. For Luther found great comfort in the fact that the Holy Spirit exercises the power of salvation through his Word in oral, written, and also sacramental forms. In Schmalkalden in 1537, he made clear that the heart of his message was that "Jesus Christ, our Lord and God, was handed over to death for our trespasses and was raised for our justification… he alone is the Lamb of God who takes away the sin of the world." Luther added: "On this doctrine stands all that we teach and practice."

Many of Luther's own students regarded him as superhuman, and admirers across the centuries have difficulty focusing on the reality of this ordinary man with great gifts. A picture of the Reformer that does not reflect what his situation was really like lessens the benefits gained from studying his life and thought. This volume enhances the reader's ability to grasp the life of this servant of God's Word and the significance of his message more fully.

Robert Kolb is Missions Professor Emeritus of Systematic Theology at the Concordia Seminary in St. Louis, Missouri

Introduction

LUTHERLAND

Easy Travel From America and Great Britain

Martin Luther, the German Reformer, spent most of his time in an area located southwest of Berlin, between Dresden and the Harz Mountains. This is the heartland of the Lutheran Church, where Philipp Melanchthon, Heinrich Schütz, and Johann Sebastian Bach also resided. In Luther's time, this was a landscape of duchies and kingdoms, most importantly Saxony, with forests, farmland, castles, monasteries, churches, and cobblestone streets, with Leipzig and Erfurt as major cities, and Wittenberg, Luther's hometown, as the seat of a new university. After World War II, the area was occupied by the US Army, which handed it over to the Soviets in July 1945, due to the Yalta Agreement. It became part of Communist East Germany. During this time, the Protestant Church was embattled. Finally in 1989, the Wall came down. Today, the states of Thuringia, Saxony, and Saxony-Anhalt have been newly formed as part of a reunited Germany. Today, this area is dubbed "Lutherland."

After reunification in 1990, the federal government of Germany and private investors poured billions of euros into these dilapidated cities, for everything from housing to hotels. Autobahns were turned from four to six lanes, new roads were paved. High-speed rail networks were constructed, like the routes from Berlin to Erfurt or Leipzig. Train stations were renovated—including the historic Central Station in Leipzig, the third largest in Europe—airports were built from scratch, hotels, restaurants, and shopping malls were established, theaters, art venues, and museums. Many of these towns with their churches, cobblestones, and castles were splendidly renovated. This makes traveling in "Lutherland" easy and convenient—and not a moment too soon, since millions of visitors are expected. It is possible to see most of it in one speedy week, although there is enough to fill four weeks. The best way to get there from the United States is to fly to either Frankfurt or Berlin. Delta, United, and Air Berlin offer direct flights to the German capital, and every major airline flies to Frankfurt. Berlin is a lot closer to the actual "Lutherland" and has quite a few interesting places to see, while Frankfurt has more flights. Leipzig-Halle has an airport as well, but no direct flights from the US. From Berlin, the route goes south to Wittenberg, Leipzig, Halle, Eisleben, Weimar, Erfurt, and Wartburg Castle near Eisenach, where Luther translated the Holy Bible into German. From Frankfurt am Main, Eisenach would be the first stop.

The first decision to make is: Will you travel by rental car, or by train? Buses are also available, and astonishingly cheap, but they only connect major cities, so they are not suitable for the whole trip. Cars are available at every airport and in every city from many rental companies, and they can be booked in advance. They can be rented at the arrival airport and dropped off at the departure airport, although the car company might charge a premium. There might also be restrictions or higher prices for seniors. Parking is not a problem outside of the downtown area in larger cities, and even there, paid parking spots are nearly always available. But gas is much more expensive than in America. Also, German Autobahns mostly don't have speed limits, which takes getting used to. Not everyone is comfortable with a BMW impatiently flashing its lights and driving 150 miles per hour a few feet behind our bumper.

Trains are a fast and safe alternative. Germany has a nationwide system of high-speed trains connecting large cities, called ICE. ICE cars have power outlets, internet (albeit a bit unreliable), and dining cars. They also are equipped with a more comfortable (and pricier) First Class with leather seats, coffee, and free newspapers. Most stations have elevators.

Traveling by ICE is not cheap, but special deals and rail passes are available. Smaller towns are connected by slower and cheaper regional trains. They run several times a day, as do the ICEs. For those regional trains, a daily pass for all of "Lutherland" is available, starting from 23 Euros for a single person (43 Euro for five people). Deutsche Bahn has an app, also in English, which lets you check trains' schedules and status.

The ICE from Frankfurt airport to Leipzig leaves about every hour or half hour during the day. In the evening, the frequency diminishes, and night trains are nearly non-existent. The Frankfurt–Leipzig route takes about three hours and thirty minutes. The train stops in Eisenach and Erfurt. From Erfurt, regional trains leave for Gotha, Weimar, and other smaller cities, and run all the way up to Leipzig (and Halle). Leipzig offers frequent connections to Dresden, the capital of Saxony, and to Halle, Magdeburg, and Berlin. About every other train from Leipzig to Berlin stops in Wittenberg. The Berlin–Leipzig route takes about one hour and fifteen minutes. Taxis area available at train stations. Fares are regulated, but higher than in America.

We don't recommend packing up every morning to move just a few miles down the road, unless you intend to replicate Luther's experience (in which case you should walk or buy a horse). Furthermore, the main attractions in "Lutherland" are Wittenberg, where Luther lived, followed by Eisleben, where he was born and died, and Eisenach with Wartburg Castle. All three places are small historic towns with limited hotel capacities. During the anniversary of the Reformation in 2017, they will be flooded with tourists from all over the world. It will be very difficult to find accommodation, if at all. If staying there is really crucial, we strongly suggest booking a room well in advance. Better yet, we suggest staying in Leipzig or Halle for a few days, if not a week, and taking day trips to the surrounding places. Both cities are major transportation hubs with many hotels, from luxury to affordable. Both cities have the atmosphere people traveling on the trail of Luther are looking for. Leipzig has major religious institutions like the Church of St. Nicholas and the Church of St. Thomas with the Bach Choir. Halle has the famous Market Church of Our Dear Ladies, Georg Friedrich Händel, museums as well, and a largely intact historic downtown that has been renovated since the Wall came down.

To explore the southern, Thuringian part of "Lutherland," we recommend staying in Erfurt, where Luther spent his early life as a monk in a monastery. Erfurt, the splendidly renovated state capital of Thuringia, has an even more medieval atmosphere, many historic buildings, and plenty of hotels and restaurants, including 4- and 5-star hotels. Weimar, Gotha, and Jena are so close to Erfurt that they would have been considered walking distance in Luther's era. Weimar to Erfurt, for instance, is fourteen minutes by commuter train.

We would also like to give some practical advice: Pack, of course, your passport, your driver's license, and money—German banks change dollars to euros, but credit cards are not commonly accepted, so we recommend carrying some cash at all times. However, you can use a credit card at most ATMs to withdraw money. Ask your bank for details. American cell phones work, but only if they are tri- or quad-band devices. Most US carriers offer international plans, but for longer stays, it might be worth buying a local call-by-call SIM card (best prices are at discount supermarkets such as Aldi). You will need to have your carrier unlock your phone, though. An adapter for power outlets will also be necessary. Not only are German power plugs shaped differently, the current is 240 volts (as opposed to 120 volts in the US). However, most devices, especially laptops, have a built-in switch for voltage.

Travel insurance is recommended, but if you get sick, it will not break the bank. And every mid-sized city has a pharmacy on night duty. Solid shoes, long pants, and at least a light jacket should be brought along, even in summer. And for Reformation Day on October 31, bundle up (then again, Wittenberg will be so overcrowded, you will warm each other!). For every shopping emergency, the main train stations in Berlin and Leipzig have been turned into shopping malls, which are also open on Sunday. They sell everything from T-shirts to toothpaste.

Since "Lutherland" was part of East Germany, not everyone speaks English, especially in smaller towns. While information in English is usually posted next to historic buildings, English brochures may not be as plentiful as desired, and at smaller train stations, guidance in English may be hard to come by. However, Berlin and Leipzig offer stores with English-language books and newspapers. Hotels also generally have internet for catching up on information. Also an East German specialty: People, and businesses, are up early in the day (but since you want to see everything, so are you).

As for food, while "Lutherland" now has the ubiquitous Chinese chain restaurants and the Golden Arches, it also has restaurants with local specialties, from Thuringian Bratwurst to German potato salad, Leipziger Allerlei, and roast boar with potato dumplings. And while grocery stores are closed on Sundays, bakeries are open. In any case, you will not go hungry. Nor will you go thirsty, because there are plenty of pubs all around—much like in the times of Martin Luther.

Eva C. Schweitzer

Traveling in Lutherland
www.visit-luther.de, www.visit-luther.com
www.saxony-anhalt-tourism.eu
www.luther2017.de/en/
www.lutherweg.de/

Train Travel and Rail Passes
www.bahn.com/i/view/USA/en
www.bahn.de/p_en/view/offers/international/german railpass.shtml?

Luther in America: Current Exhibits
Minneapolis: *new.artsmia.org/luther*
New York: *themorgan.org/exhibitions/word-and-image*
Los Angeles: *www.lacma.org*

Luther Year 2017: Special Events

A sample of major Luther Year events. More at:
www.visit-luther.com/explore-luthercountry/events/2017-500th-anniversary-of-the-Reformation/

36th German Evangelical Church Convention 2017
May 24–28, 2017, Berlin and Wittenberg

The German Evangelical Church Convention will offer Christians of all confessions from the whole world over 2000 events at various locations in Berlin and Wittenberg from May 24–28 for watching, listening, and joining. One highlight will be the outdoor service in Wittenberg on May 28 at noon.

More at: *www.kirchentag.de/english.html*

Special Events in Berlin
The Luther Effect, April 12–November 5, 2017
Martin-Gropius-Bau, Niederkirchnerstr. 7, 10963 Berlin

The Deutsches Historisches Museum presents "The Luther Effect," an exhibit telling a global story of effect and counter-effect of the Reformation. It brings together outstanding exponents, many of which have never before been displayed in Germany. More at:

www.dhm.de/en/ausstellungen/preview/the-luther-effect.html

Special Events in Leipzig
Kirchentag (Church Convention) on the Way:
May 25–28, 2017
Church of St. Thomas and all over town in Leipzig

"Music. Dispute. Life." will be the theme of the "Kirchentag on the Way." In 1519, Leipzig was the scene of the Disputation. Almost 500 years later, it will be out on the streets of Leipzig again. Visitors will be able to listen to the music of Johann Sebastian Bach, the St. Thomas Boys Choir, and trombone bands, in the spirit of "The Sound of Leipzig."

The Museum of the Printing Arts presents "Luther and Printing" from May–September 2017. The Stadtgeschichtliches Museum in the Old Town Hall has a Luther Exhibit as well.

More at: *r2017.org/en/kirchentage-on-the-way/leipzig*

Special Events in Wittenberg
Reformation Festival (Reformationsfest), October 31, 2017
Castle Church, City Church, Market Square
Wittenberg stages a Reformation Day festival, starting with services in the Castle Church and St. Mary's Church. The cobblestone streets come alive with a parade, theater, concerts and exhibitions. 200,000 people are expected. In the week before, the Renaissance Music Festival takes place, with concerts, dancing, and the Renaissance Ball.

More at: *www.wittenberger-reformationsfest.de*

Luther! 95 Treasures—95 People, May 13–Nov. 5, 2017
Augusteum, Collegienstr. 54, 06886 Wittenberg
The exhibition sheds light on Luther's family life with Katharina von Bora. It also features an impressive presentation of his activities, complete with Bible prints, manuscripts, Cranach paintings, and more. It also introduces "95 People," each with their own relationship to Luther, personalities from the 16th to the 21st centuries, from all over the world. More at

www.lutherstadt-wittenberg.de/en, www.3xhammer.de/en

Special Events at Wartburg Castle
Luther and the Germans, May 4–November 5, 2017
Auf der Wartburg 1, 99817 Eisenach
The presentation sheds light on Luther as a nationally symbolic personality. Reformation topics will be introduced, creating a bridge between Luther's point of view and the present.

More at: *www.luther.de/en/wartburg.html*

Special Events in Torgau
Katharina-Tag and Castle Church Festival, all year
Castle Hartenfels and other places
Torgau has a multitude of exhibits, concerts, street fairs, and services, including a "Katharina-Tag" on the weekend of June 24–25, accompanied by a week of church music, a Bible Fest devoted to Elector John Frederick I in September, and a festival for the anniversary of the dedication of the Castle Church on October 8. More at:

www.tic-torgau.de/content/lutherdekade-veranstaltungen.html

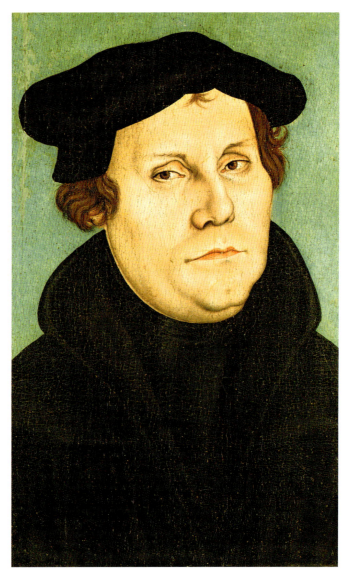

Martin Luther, *painted by Lucas Cranach the Elder, in Lutherstadt Wittenberg. The German Reformer who stood up against indulgences, set the Reformation in motion, and changed the history of the world.*

Chapter One

Luther's Uprising

Ninety-Five Theses and the Pope: How the Reformation Began

It was October 31, 1517, now 500 years ago, when Martin Luther made history: He affixed the Ninety-five Theses to the door of the Castle Church in Wittenberg, the town where he lived and preached. Luther was Catholic, as was everyone in Europe at that time, a priest, and a professor of Theology. The event itself is somewhat disputed; some doubt that it happened at all, but Philipp Melanchthon, his friend and also a professor in Wittenberg, was a witness.

However, Luther did not angrily swing a hammer. The door of the impressive Castle Church served as a bulletin board for the city's theologians. It is also public record that Luther wrote a—submissive and respectful—letter to Albert, the Archbishop of the German town of Mainz. The letter was about the same issue as the theses—indulgences, *Ablasshandel*. Indulgences were monies paid to the Church, who then made sure the sinner would go to heaven. Luther resented the sale of indulgences, because the remission of sins was being mixed up with political and economic goals.

But it was not just about money; indulgences were a reflection of an international power play, with the Archbishop of Mainz, Saxon Elector Frederick the Wise (see page 58), and the Pope in Rome as major players. Luther, so to speak, lived in the very last trenches of the Roman Empire: The Holy Roman Empire of the German Nation, an ensemble of kingdoms, mos importantly Northern Italy, Burgundy in France, Bohemia with Prague as the capital, and the Kingdom of Germany. The latter consisted of many duchies, including

Saxony, which covered present-day Saxony, and parts of Thuringia and Saxony-Anhalt. Elector Frederick the Wise became a life-long benefactor of Luther. Frederick did this for political, not religious reasons. He wanted to strengthen the German princes against the Pope in Rome.

One German duchy was Mainz, then the largest archbishopric in Christianity—and also the seat of the archchancellor of Germany, the head of the German Electors. Because the archbishopric had changed occupants three times between 1504 and 1514, it had to pay a triple fee to Rome for the appointment of a new archbishop and for the granting of a gallium (the symbol for the rank of archbishop). The price tag was 10,000 ducats or 14,000 guilders (one guilder being somewhat more than fifty dollars today).

Hence, the archbishopric was in extreme debt. When a new archbishop was due to be elected, a nobleman was sought who would have the necessary finances at his disposal. Enter aforementioned Albert of Hohenzollern-Brandenburg, who had been the archbishop of Magdeburg since 1513. Even though holding multiple offices was prohibited, Rome still permitted it after a special dispensation was negotiated, plus a payment of 21,000 ducats or 29,000 guilders.

Because Albert did not have this amount at his disposal after all, he turned to the Fugger Bank of Augsburg. In return, Albert had to permit the selling of the so-called "St. Peter's Indulgence" to pay for the construction of St. Peter's Basilica in Rome. The other half of the proceeds would go to the Fugger Bank to repay the debt. From the outset, there was an obvious intertwining of religious and financial interests.

Indulgences were to be sold for a period of eight years in the ecclesiastical provinces of Mainz, Magdeburg, and Brandenburg. With few exceptions, they would apply to all sins. Consequently, "sub-commissioners," preachers of indulgence, and confessors were recruited to execute the campaign. On January 22, 1517, Johann Tetzel—a Dominican monk from Leipzig—was sworn in as general sub-commissioner for the sale of indulgences in the province of Magdeburg.

On April 10 of that same year, Tetzel was in Jüterbog, a town near Wittenberg. For the first time, Luther was directly confronted with the effects of the "St. Peter's Indulgence." Initially, Luther tried to clarify the matter in his sermons. Luther was not criticizing the practice of indulgences per se.

Pope Leo X

Leo X (Giovanni de Medici), Pope during Luther's time from March 11, 1513, to December 1, 1521, imposed the bull of excommunication against the Reformer. De Medici, of the powerful and influencial Medici family, studied theology and canon law in Pisa. At the instigation of his father, he was promoted to cardinal in 1489, and bolstered his family in Florence. After the Medici were driven from Florence —mainly by Girolamo Savonarola, a Dominican friar— he resided in France, Germany, and Flanders, until he returned to Rome after the death of Alexander VI (1503). In 1511, Pope Julius II sent him to Bologna and Romagna. That same year, he was appointed commander-in-chief of the Spanish and papal troops in the war against France.

Leo was not very lucky in foreign policy. When the Emperor was to be elected in 1519, Leo first supported French King Francis I, then Saxon Elector Frederick the Wise, and finally Spanish King Charles I. Charles I later became head of the Holy Roman Empire, until 1556—as Emperor Charles V. In 1521, Leo formed an alliance with Charles V against France. True to his election promises, Leo summoned a general council, the Fifth Lateran Council (1513–17), which brought no noteworthy results, despite beneficial decrees for reform. Above all, the lack of true reform was because both the Pope and curia lacked any serious intention for the renewal of the Church.

In this Erfurt building at Allerheiligenstrasse 11, the first letter of indulgence issued in the city was printed in 1473.

Rather, he was concerned about misunderstandings, saying buyers of indulgences were being tricked into believing that from that day forward they could be sure of their salvation and that their souls would arrive in heaven as soon as the money was paid—referring to Tetzel's rhyme, "As soon as a coin in the coffer rings / the soul from purgatory springs." Luther was upset by the claim that people could supposedly be forgiven—even of grave sin—by means of indulgences. So, Luther sent his cover letter to Albert, the Archbishop of Mainz, and included the Ninety-five Theses, which criticized indulgences from a number of different angles. In his discussion of his Theses, Luther had always—incorrectly—assumed that the Pope shared his opinion concerning indulgences. Even in 1541, Luther emphasized that he initially did not intend to oppose indulgences per se—just their misuse.

He most certainly did not want to oppose the Pope. But he was mistaken. Frederick the Wise of Saxony knew better. He had his Court Preacher Georg Spalatin (page 56) read Luther's Theses to him. Frederick commented, "Mark my words. The Pope will not be able to tolerate that."

The Theses were intensely discussed within the Church, and Luther had to write an explanation of them in 1518. Luther had two tasks before him: first, the difficult and almost hopeless confrontation with the ecclesiastical system and, second, building up and implementing his new realization. The court case against Luther was opened in Rome in summer 1518. Frederick the Wise, however, managed to arrange for Luther to be summoned not to Rome but to Augsburg, before Cardinal Cajetan. That hearing would take place on October 12 and 14 in the Fugger House (Fuggerhaus) in that city. Cajetan asked Luther to recant and threatened him and his supporters with excommunication. In a loud shouting match, Luther refused to recant. Apparently, friends then helped Luther to pass through an unguarded city gate to make a quick escape to Wittenberg, riding the first leg of the journey—to Nuremberg—bareback.

After Augsburg, a moratorium followed. Luther, however, was eager for another debate. Soon, the Leipzig Debate with the theology professor Johann Eck would give him just that opportunity. The Disputation of Leipzig was a huge, well-attended event. Luther regarded himself as the winner, but so did Eck. Eck asked the Pope to move against Luther for holding to "Hussite heresy." The Hussites were an early Reformation movement in Bohemia; their founder, Jan Hus, was burned at the stake in 1415, followed by the Hussite wars.

Accordingly, a bull threatening Luther and his followers with excommunication was posted in Meissen, Merseburg, and Brandenburg in September 1520. As a result, Luther's books were burned in several cities. Luther reacted to this on December 10, 1520, in Wittenberg—by publicly burning papal books and the canon law, along with the bull threatening his excommunication.

Clothing in Luther's Day

Even before the Reformation era, clothing indicated social status. Only the aristocracy could afford expensive colors, such as purple (from a snail known as the spiny dye-murex) or carmine (from insects). This was also true of decorations and rare materials such as silk. The lower classes wore linen, hemp, untreated cotton, or wool. Some of those materials were dyed with colors extracted from plants. Farmers and day laborers usually made their own clothing, while the nobility or clerics purchased their clothes with money gained from taxes.

In the Middle Ages, men wore linen underwear and wool cloaks, fastened with a belt. Over this they wore a square cloak fastened on the right side with a clasp. Men also wore felt hats and kept their legs warm with long stockings pulled above shoes made from sewn leather.

Women wore long linen undergarments with long sleeves under an ankle-length garment, covered by a cape that closed over the chest. Women's head coverings were made from linen and were about one to almost three inches wide; on top of these were placed small, flat bonnets or veils. Noble women wore richly decorated turban-style head coverings. Shoes were pointed and made from soft, decorated leather. As it had been the fashion in Roman times, women often bleached their hair blond.

Over the course of time, fashions differentiated according to regions. For instance, beginning in the 15th century, townspeople wore shoes with wooden soles, which protected their feet from mud and moisture.

Luther complained about the obsession of both the rich and the poor with their clothing. "Do we not all know endless stories about how much time and money people spend on their clothing? Therefore, it should no longer be called simply a desire or an overindulgence, but rather foolishness for them to adorn themselves with so much clothing and jewelry—like donkeys that are born to lug around gold."

On December 10, 1520, Luther wrote to Spalatin:

"On December 10, 1520, at nine o'clock in the morning, all these books of the Pope will be burned in Wittenberg in front of the eastern gate, near the Church of the Holy Cross: the *Decretum*, the *Decretals*, the *Liber Sextus*, the *Clementines*, the *Extravagantes*, and the newest bull of Leo X… as well as several other [texts] that were added by various others so that the Papist arsonists can see that it does not take much to burn books they cannot refute."

Many years later, in 1541, Luther still wrote indignantly about the practice of indulgences:

"Meanwhile, I found out what dreadful and abominable articles Tetzel was preaching, and I will mention some of them now: He claimed that he had such grace and power from the Pope that even if someone seduced the Holy Virgin Mary, the Mother of God, or impregnated her, Tetzel could forgive that person, if only he placed the proper amount in the money chest. Similarly, Tetzel claimed that when the red indulgence-cross bearing the papal arms is lifted up in church, it is just as powerful as the cross of Christ.… And again, that if anyone puts money in the chest for a soul in purgatory, the soul flies [from purgatory] to heaven as soon as the coin falls and rings at the bottom. Tetzel claimed that the grace from indulgences is the same grace as the grace through which a man is reconciled to God."

Luther wrote several books against the papacy. The best-known is *Christ and Antichrist*, in which Luther comments crassly on ten equally crass caricatures of the Pope. On the occasion of the Council that convened in Trent in March 1545, a text of Luther's was published, *Against the Roman Papacy, an Institution of the Devil*. In it, he describes the Pope as the "antichrist and werewolf, as an enemy of God, an enemy of Christ, and an enemy of all Christians and the whole world," and he warns that anyone who follows the Pope must know "that he is obedient to the devil in opposition to God."

The Ninety-Five Theses of Dr. Martin Luther (A Selection)

Out of love for the truth and in zeal to ascertain it, the following Theses will be publicly discussed at Wittenberg under the chairmanship of the Reverend Father Martin Luther, Master of Arts and Sacred Theology, and regularly appointed professor there. Therefore, he requests that those who cannot be present to debate orally with us will do so by letter. In the name of our Lord Jesus Christ. Amen.

1. When our Lord and Master Jesus Christ said, "Repent" (Matt. 4:17), He meant that the entire life of a believer should be one of repentance.

5. The Pope neither intends nor is able to remit any penalties except those that he has imposed, based on his own decrees or those of the ecclesiastical canons.

21. Therefore, indulgence preachers are in error when they say that a man is free and rid of every punishment by means of papal indulgences.

24. Therefore, unavoidably, the majority of people are completely deceived by those promises boastfully given for the remission of punishments.

27. A man-made teaching is being preached when someone claims that as soon as the money rings in the coffer, a soul flies up (out of purgatory).

28. To be sure, as soon as the money rings in the coffer, profits and greed can increase, but the intercession of the Church is based on God's will alone.

32. Whoever believes that he can be certain of his salvation because of a letter of indulgence will be eternally damned, along with his teachers.

35. It is a non-Christian teaching when someone claims that contrition is not necessary for those who ransom their souls (from purgatory) or for those who purchase letters of absolution.

36. Any Christian who truly repents is entitled to the full remission of punishments and guilt, even without a letter of indulgence.

37. Any true Christian, whether living or dead, partakes in all the blessings of Christ and of the Church that are given to him by God—even without a letter of indulgence.

45. Christians should be taught that whoever sees someone in need, goes past him, and instead pays for indulgences is not buying an indulgence from the Pope. Rather, these people will receive the wrath of God.

46. Christians should be taught that whoever does not live in affluence should hold on to the necessities for his household and under no circumstances should squander money on indulgences.

50. Christians should be taught that if the Pope knew the coercive methods of the indulgence preachers, he would rather see St. Peter's Basilica reduced to ashes than have it built with the skin, flesh, and bones of his sheep.

51. Christians are to be taught that it would be the Pope's wish—as his duty—to give of his own money to very many of those from whom certain hawkers of pardons cajole money, even if the Church of St. Peter might have to be sold.

52. It is vain to expect salvation on the basis of a letter of indulgence, even if the (indulgence) commissioner in fact, even if the Pope himself pledged his own soul for it.

62. The true treasury of the Church is the Holy Gospel of the glory and grace of God.

92. Therefore, away with all those prophets who preach to Christians, "Peace! Peace!" when there is no peace!

93. May it go well with every prophet who preaches to Christians, "Cross! Cross!" when there is no cross!

94. Christians should be encouraged to strive to follow Christ—their Head—through punishments, death, and hell.

95. They should trust to enter the kingdom of heaven through many tribulations rather themselves in false spiritual security.

Wittenberg, with a view of the twin towers of St. Mary's City Church, where Luther preached and got married. One of the town's many outdoor restaurants is next to a historc well. The town still has cobblestone streets.

Chapter Two

Luther's Town

Lutherstadt Wittenberg, Birthplace of the Reformation

Wittenberg, a town between Berlin and Leipzig, was Martin Luther's hometown, where the historic events took place that shook the foundations of Christianity. In Wittenberg, Luther and his colleagues at the newly founded Leucorea University found the spiritual environment that put him in a position to unleash monumental forces, and change the world. Today, Lutherstadt Wittenberg is Luther Central! Practically every spot is associated with the Reformer.

The rise of Wittenberg began when Saxony Elector Frederick III, also known Frederick the Wise, founded the Leucorea University of Saxony (leucos means "white" and refers to "Wittenberg," which means "white mountain"). The university celebrated its opening on October 18, 1502, and would become the university where Martin Luther taught and developed his theses. Luther was asked to be a professor at Leucorea in 1510, and his friend and companion Philipp Melanchthon would join the faculty in 1519.

In the early 13th century, universities had been founded elsewhere under the authority of the Pope. They taught the Aristotelian academic methods customary in the Middle Ages, as well as Roman law in the area of jurisprudence. But over time, secular powers (kings, princes, and cities), began to found universities as well. With that, non-theological subjects were beginning to grow in their independence and significance. This was also the case at the Leucorea.

In the beginning, there was still a medieval aura to the Leucorea, St. Augustine was chosen as its patron saint and each department was appointed its own saint. To determine the correct seating order at staff meetings, the various faculties were ranked. As usual in the Late Middle Ages, the theological department sat at the head of the table, followed by the law and medical faculties in less prominent positions. At the bottom of the ranking was the arts faculty. One new regulation, however, indicated the spirit of rising humanism: crowned poets (*poetae laureati*), were now ranked with the masters of arts faculty. These poets represented German humanism. They dealt in new ways with the ancient languages—Greek, Latin, and Hebrew.

The university required a large amount of teaching material for its students—printing had been invented by Johannes Gutenberg in 1439—so printers moved to town. Wittenberg's first printed texts were produced the same year the university was founded. The prior of the Augustinian Monastery was Johann von Staupitz (page 56), who would become a defender of the Reformation. Frederick the Wise also assigned two Augustinian Hermits as professors, one in the theological faculty, the other in the arts faculty, who lectured on moral philosophy. With professors and students moving into town, and printers being busy, the economy grew. The city of Wittenberg supported the Leucorea as much as possible. For instance, the confession house at the Franciscan Monastery was restored for the arts faculty's lectures.

The foundation of the Leucorea also compelled changes in Wittenberg's municipal planning. Because student accommodations were scarce, some students had to live in private homes. In 1504, a law was passed, requiring anyone owning or inheriting an empty lot to build a structure on that property within one year. So the Leucorea caused Wittenberg's first building boom of the 16th century as well. Buildings were constructed on vacant lots; homes were expanded to include small businesses for craftsmen or merchants. Even professors took in students, as did Luther and his wife, Katharina. This is when the houses now located around the City Church were built, separating the church from the city hall.

WITTENBERG IN THE LATE MIDDLE AGES

The town was first documented as "burchwardum wittenburg" in 1180. After 1200, it belonged to the ruling Ascanians. In 1260, Albrecht II established his residence there, and in 1293, he gave Wittenberg the rights of a city. In 1356, Wittenberg became the residence of the Elector, and had a high court beginning in 1441. Wittenberg at that time was known only as a regional trade center for shoe- and cloth makers, butchers, and bakers. Of the 356 homeowners paying property tax, 172 had the right to brew beer. The remaining 184 were so-called *Buddelinge*, owning tiny homes.

Wittenberg was fortified with eleven towers, three of which have been preserved to this day. They remain around its three gated towers: the Elbe Gate to the south, the Coswig Gate (also known as Castle Gate) to the west, and the Elster Gate to the east.

Securing water was a problem in the Middle Ages, when the only water supply was from streams diverted into town, from which people drew their drinking water. But raw sewage was also disposed in these streams, which then flowed into the Elbe River. Beer brewers complained about the poor water quality and the few wells that had been dug, which were not providing enough water.

In 1542, Elector John Frederick commissioned Mayor Philipp Reichenbach and District Magistrate Christoph Gross to construct a system of piped water, which would supply the Elector's castle and the fortress of Wittenberg with sufficient water. Part of this can still be seen today, e.g. in the Cranach Courtyard.

Frederick the Wise also commissioned the castle with the Castle Church. The castle of the Ascanians formerly at that site had been torn down already, and the new castle with two wings was completed in 1509. Construction cost 32,466 guilders, thirteen groschen, and nine pfennigs. The Castle Church formed the third wing of the residential castle. The

Castle Church became the University Church. Elections for various university offices were held in the sacristy, while the sanctuary served as the main hall of the Leucorea. And its door was used as a "bulletin board" for academic theses.

The Castle Church was constructed with a high altar painted by Lucas Cranach the Elder, another famed resident of Wittenberg. One of Cranach's works still hanging in the Church today is *The Martyrdom of St. Catherine*. On the side wings was a depiction of six female saints, known as the "Princes' Altar of Dessau" (*Dessauer Fürstenaltar*). Today this painting is exhibited in Dessau's Georgium Castle in the Anhalt Art Gallery (*Anhaltischen Gemäldegalerie*). Also, world-famous painter Albrecht Dürer contributed works that were originally in the Castle Church, of which four are preserved. Two altarpiece panels depict the *Seven Joys of the Virgin* and the *Seven Sorrows of the Virgin*. The panel depicting the seven sorrows is now in Dresden, while the *Virgin* is displayed in the Alte Pinakothek in Munich. By continuously sponsoring Masses, the Elector filled the church with spiritual life. In one year, 1,138 Masses were sung and 7,856 Masses were read.

When Frederick the Wise died, the Castle Church lost its importance. His brother John the Steadfast, who succeeded him, positioned himself more clearly on the side of the Reformation and closed the Allerheiligenstift in 1525. Under a cloud of secrecy, the collection of relics was brought to the city of Torgau. Georg Goldschmidt separated the gold, silver, jewels, and pearls they contained and reworked them into items of daily use. The silver was sold to Nuremberg, with a profit of 24,739 guilders, A few items were preserved, however, such as a drinking glass owned by St. Elizabeth of Thuringia. Today it can be viewed in Coburg Castle (Veste Coburg).

In 1760, the Castle Church was destroyed in the Seven-Years'-War. The only items from inside the original church that survived were the tomb figures of Frederick the Wise and John the Steadfast. In 1892, the church was renovated in the neo-Gothic style. The aim was to have a building presenting the main Reformers. Statues commemorating Luther and his most important allies were placed inside: Justus Jonas, Johannes Bugenhagen, Nikolaus von Amsdorf, Urbanus Rhegius, Georg Spalatin, Philipp Melanchthon, Johannes Brenz, and Caspar Cruciger. On the ceiling are the seals of towns that sided with the Reformation. Of the original 198 seals, 128 are preserved. On the walls are the Reformers' coats of arms. The pulpit features the four Gospel writers, plus additional coats of arms of cities that played a major role in Luther's life: Eisleben, Erfurt, Wittenberg, and Worms.

The balcony displays fifty-two coats of arms of the noblemen who dealt with Luther during the first half of the 16th century. This rich collection illustrates the intention of Crown Prince Frederick William III (who later became Emperor Frederick III), to embellish the Castle Church as a "sanctuary for all of Protestant Christianity." The only features of the Renaissance-era castle structure itself that remain today are the magnificent stairwells. They lead nowhere, because the original building had three stories, but a fourth was added when the church was transformed into a Prussian fortress.

Martin Luther's grave in the Castle Church in Wittenberg. Philipp Melanchthon is also buried there.

The focal point of Luther's life was the former Augustinian Monastery. Referring to the black cowls its resident monks wore, it was also known as the Black Abbey. It was located near the Elster Gate, south of the city wall, where the Holy Ghost Hospital (Heilig-Geist-Spital) had originally been.

Johann von Staupitz founded the monastery in 1502, but was not able to complete it to include a church and cloistered courtyard as originally planned. He had, however, a monastic house constructed, with lecture halls for the university on the second floor and accommodations for forty monks on the third floor. At any given time, fifteen to twenty monks from out of town lived here while attending the university.

Luther lived in this monastery for a while, too, though he probably did his reading and writing in the dining room in the evening, where Cranach's *Ten Commandments* panel can be viewed today. Later, Luther and his family lived on the second floor, but because of countless renovations over the centuries, we no longer have the exact floor plan.

THE AUGUSTINIANS

The Order of the Augustinian Hermits was established in the mid-13th century by order of Pope Alexander IV, who decreed that several groups of hermits living in communities in Italy join together and form the Order of Hermits of St. Augustine (*www.augustiner.de*).

Even in Luther's day, the order was considered to be very strict. The Augustinian monks rose every morning at 3 a.m., with a short prayer service dedicated to St. Mary, followed by a long service of prayers and readings called Matins. This service was followed by others: Prime (6 a.m.), Terce (9 a.m.), Sext (noon), None and Vespers (early afternoon), and Compline (before bed).

The daily Mass for the monastery was celebrated in the morning. Hymns to St. Mary ("Ave Maria" and "Salve Regina") were sung after every prayer service. Every monk was required to sing these services..

Naturally, Luther's large home with its numerous occupants could not be run without servants. Luther had his own servant, Wolf Seberger, who received a small salary from the Elector. Seberger was responsible for purchasing supplies, tending the garden, and running the household. Luther regarded him as good-natured but often complained about his laziness.

In addition to Luther House, Luther and his wife also ran a small farm, Zülsdorf. The farm provided food for the Luther household. Luther's "Katie" also received gifts from friends, such as fish, game, wine, and beer. However, shortages occasionally forced Luther to go without beer—once even for a period of forty days in summer 1540.

But that could not make Luther angry. What did make him angry toward the end of his life, however, was the way many people despised God's Word. This attitude led to immoral behavior among the population, which became obvious in the way the women of Wittenberg wore dresses that were too short and too low in the neck. For that reason, Luther wrote to Katie on July 28, 1545, from the town of Zeitz:

"To my dear wife and manager of our household, Katharina von Bora—'preacher,' beer brewer, gardener, and whatever else you may be—grace and peace. Dear Katie, [our son] Hans will tell you all about our trip… I wish I could avoid returning to Wittenberg. My heart has grown so cold that I no longer enjoy being there. I would like you to sell our garden and plot, our house and yard. Also, I would like to return that big house to my dearest lord, the Elector. It would be best for you to move to Zülsdorf while I am alive. I imagine my salary would help you to improve our little farm… I cannot believe how women—both old and young—in Wittenberg are starting to expose themselves in front and in back and that there is no one around who would punish them or try to prevent this behavior! By doing that, God's Word is scorned."

Luther did not return to Wittenberg until the Elector, the city, and the university promised to address the situation.

FOOD AND DRINK IN THE MIDDLE AGES

In Luther's day, nourishment depended on social status and on the time of the year. On feast days, or in autumn after a fruitful summer, or when animals were butchered, food was abundant. Crop failures, however, caused famines and drove up prices in the regional marketplaces when seed grain was unavailable. Because of reduced planting after a crop failure, another meager harvest would often follow. Above all, it was the poor peasants and serfs who were affected by crop failures, because they had to offer payment in kind and were thus unable to purchase food for themselves. Only when potatoes from South America were introduced would this vicious cycle be broken.

Game, poultry, beef, wine, and even wheat bread were reserved for the nobility and rich feudal lords, and spices and raw sugar were luxury items. The basic sweetener for common folk was honey. Simple peasants had to be content with oat bread, rye bread, and beer. Nevertheless, Luther observed that, "Although they do not live as magnificently as kings and princes, the common people still enjoy the best goods, such as peace and tranquility. They also live much more securely and blissfully within their fences than kings and princes do in their castles or fortresses."

Luther also occasionally remarked how dark bread, meat, and beer tasted better to peasants after their hard work than white bread, game, and wine tasted to princes.

Since the 13th century, writings on proper table manners (*Tischzucht*), informed people about proper behavior at the table. For instance, these rules stipulated that knives should not be scraped off against boots or that people should not blow their noses on tablecloths.

Picture right: Luther had already frequented the Black Bear restaurant in Wittenberg.

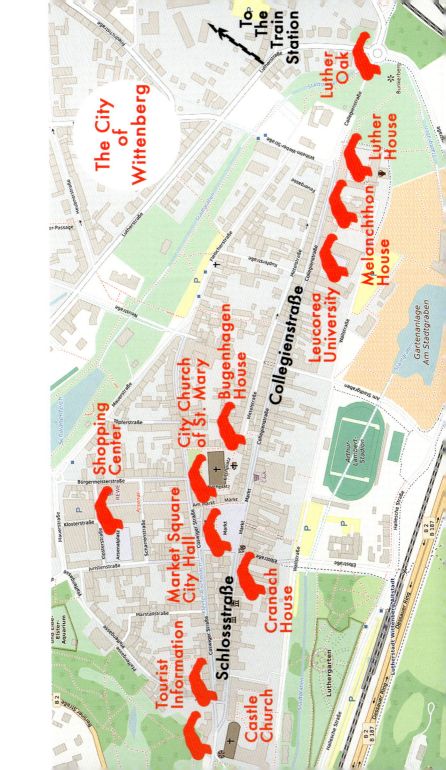

SIGHTS IN WITTENBERG

Wittenberg is designed for easy walking. The old town between the train station in the east and the Castle Church in the west is laid out along Mittelstrasse and pedestrian-only Collegienstrasse, which turns into Schlossstrasse west of Market Square. Twice a year, the old town turns into a medieval village with music, costumes, food, wine and beer, dancing, juggling and processions. October 31 (when the 95 Theses were posted), is the Reformation Fest, with classical concerts, plays, seminars and church services. Guided tours start at the tourist information center next to the Castle Church.

Castle Church with the Ninety-Five Theses Door

This is the door where Luther posted his ninety-five Theses. The original door was destroyed in the Seven Years' War of 1756–1763. But the historical event was memorialized in 1858 by a new "Theses Door" made from bronze engraved with all of Luther's theses. The church itself, where Luther preached, was also severely damaged during the wars following the Reformation, but it was rebuilt each time. In 2015, it was newly renovated. When Luther died, he was buried in the church, right under the pulpit. Melanchthon is buried across the aisle.

Castle Church Tower (Schlosskirche)

The church is part of the City Castle, and the castle tower rises high above Wittenberg. You can climb the circular stone stairs for a great view. Open daily from noon to 4 p.m.

Something cool: English services are conducted on Saturday evenings at 5 p.m., at either this church or the City Church. You can sing Luther's famous hymn, *"A Mighty Fortress is Our God,"* in English, in his very church.

www.wittenberg-english-ministry.com

Schlossstrasse and Market Square (Marktplatz)

Pastel-colored buildings from mainly the 16th and 17th centuries line this street, along with restaurants serving hearty German cuisine. In summer, many of them have outdoor tables. A narrow creek, recently unearthed, follows the street.

In Luther's time, the houses looked different. Many had timber frames exposing their clay and wood construction.

City Hall (Rathaus)

During the Reformation, Wittenberg prospered. Soon, the town outgrew the old City Hall. Beginning in 1523 (in Luther's day), it was expanded and renovated.

Court decisions were rendered outside the main door, and executions were carried out in front of the portal. The cobblestone Market Square still reveals traces of where the gallows once stood. After the proclamation of the sentence, the "sinner's bell" was rung. It sounded for the last time on May 9, 1834, when Ernst Wollkopf, a butcher's apprentice, was convicted of murder and broken on the wheel.

Wittenberg's City Hall also served other purposes. For instance, the cellar once contained a tavern (Ratskeller), as well as a jail. Cloth- and shoemakers used to sell their products in the public hall (Bürgersaal).

Luther Monument (Lutherdenkmal)

Designed by Johann Gottfried Schadow, Wittenberg's Luther Monument is one of the largest bronze statues in Germany. It stands in front of City Hall on Market Square (photo above). The monument was presented to the citizens in 1821, a very early date for a Luther monument. Eisleben did not install a Luther monument until 1883, for the 400th anniversary of the Reformer's birth, designed by Rudolf Siemering.

Cranach Courtyard at Schlossstrasse 1 (Cranachhof)

Lucas Cranach (the Elder) came to Wittenberg as a court painter in 1505, at age thirty-two. He became one of the most accomplished artists of the 16th century, and is still exhibited in many museums all over Europe. He painted well-known figures of the Reformation—including Martin Luther, who became his good friend—as well as many local princes and princesses. Due to his commercial success, he was able to purchase this courtyard in 1517–18, then the largest edifice in Wittenberg. It is now a museum, devoted to Cranach.

Cranach's House at Markt 3–4 (Cranachhaus)

This was Lucas Cranach the Elder's first house, artist studio, and print shop, bought in 1515, when he got married. His son, Lucas Cranach the Younger, was born here. In 1520, Cranach established a pharmacy (Apotheke), which is still in business. Cranach also served on the City Council, was Mayor of Wittenberg for seven years, and one of the richest citizens.

City Church of St. Mary
(Stadtkirche St. Marien)

In this lovely old church on Kirchplatz, with its double towers high above town, Martin Luther and fellow Reformer Johannes Bugenhagen gave many sermons. This is also the church where the first Mass in the German language was held and where the Lord's Supper was first administered to the congregation in "both kinds," with both bread and wine. Hence, St. Mary's is considered the "mother church" of the Reformation.

The City Church of St. Mary was first documented in 1187. The chancel and southern nave were added in 1280. Additional enhancements were made in the 15th century. In 1522, almost the entire interior was destroyed as a result of the iconoclasm triggered by Reformer Andreas Bodenstein. Seeking to prevent further damage, Luther returned from Wartburg Castle and delivered his famous Invocavit sermons here. Luther and Katharina von

Bora were married here, and their marriage is re-enacted annually in a popular street fair. All of Luther's children were baptized in the church. A large painting above the altar, by Lucas Cranach the Elder, shows Luther receiving the Last Supper. The church is open to the public, also on weekdays. Next to the Stadtkirche is the much smaller Chapel of St. Mary (photo left).

Along with the ensuing expansions of 1280, a so-called "Jewish Sow" (*Judensau*), made of stone, was placed on the southeastern corner. Similar anti-Semitic monuments are depicted at several churches in Europe. Luther also wrote a heavily anti-Semitic book, *About the Jews and Their Lies.*

After 1933, the book was re-published and widely distributed by the Nazis and the German Church. After several years of discussion about what to do with the infamous "Jewish Sow," a plaster monument was unveiled on the ground on November 11, 1988 (photo above). It is meant to communicate to Jews that Christians do not deny their guilty past. The text reads, "God's real name / The despised Shem Hamphoras / which Jews even before Christians / regarded as almost unspeakable / died with six million Jews / under the sign of the cross." Below this statement is a quote in Hebrew from Psalm 130: "Out of the depths I cry to you, O Lord!"

Bugenhagen House (Bugenhagenhaus)

A house next to the City Church was the parsonage of St. Mary's. Luther's fellow Reformer, Johannes Bugenhagen, lived here until his death in 1558. Today, the house is a museum. A bust of Bugenhagen is in front of the building, in a small park.

Wittenberg University (Universität Wittenberg)

The university has been located at Collegienstrasse since Luther's time. The gate of the structure still dates back to that period, while the rest is newer. Luther himself worked within these walls. His quotations are displayed in the entrance hall.

Melanchthon House (Melanchthonhaus)

This building on Collegienstrasse was purchased by Reformer Philipp Melanchthon in 1520, on the occasion of his wedding. In 1536, when it had become derelict, Elector John Frederick gave Melanchthon a new house. This Renaissance-era building is now a museum as well.

Luther House (Lutherhaus), Luther's Residence

Martin Luther used this former cloister, the "Black Abbey," as a residence from 1508. It was given to him by Elector August of Saxony, who supported the Reformation. Luther's wife, Katharina von Bora, moved in with him when they were married in 1525, and she basically ran the whole estate while he wrote and taught. Six children, various relatives, a couple of students, and many visitors lived on the premises as well. Luther, who was known for his eloquent yet blunt way of speaking, invited students to be present during his evening talks at the dinner table. They took notes and later published "thousands" of his comments in a book called *Table Talk*.

Luther House has been a museum since 1883. It maintains

Luther's living rooms in their original state and has artifacts from that period, including chests used for collecting money for indulgences, an "indulgence" letter, and Luther's pulpit. Lucas Cranach's fascinating painting of the *Ten Commandments* is located on wood panels. *The Wicked Deeds* are presented in quasi-cartoon style for the faithful to ponder.

Luther's Oak (Luther-Eiche)

In 1520, Martin Luther's supporters piled up a stack of Church doctrine texts and set them on fire. Luther threw in the Papal Bull, the document threatening him with excommunication unless he recanted his writings. On December 10, 1520, an oak tree was planted where the burning took place, on the corner of Lutherstrasse and Dresdner Strasse, at the entrance to the old town. The original tree, however, no longer exists. The tree currently at the site was planted in 1830.

How to get to Wittenberg:

Wittenberg is located on the Elbe River. less than one hour by car or train from Berlin and Leipzig.

By Car: Take Autobahn A9 Berlin–Nürnberg to exit 8 (Coswig), and then B187 to Wittenberg Zentrum.

By Train: The train station is a ten-minute walk east of old town (taxis are also available). From Hauptbahnhof, turn left and walk down the hill to the first traffic circle. Turn right, and you will be right at the Luther House.

Hotels in Wittenberg

Hotel Goldener Adler ***
Markt, D-06886 Wittenberg
Phone: +49 (0) 3491-43 31 30
www.goldeneradler-wittenberg.de

Hotel Schwarzer Bär ***
Schlossstrasse 2, D-06886 Wittenberg
Phone: +49 (0) 3491-42 04 34 4
www.stadthotel-wittenberg.de

Hotel Alte Canzley ***
Schlossplatz 3-5, D-06886 Wittenberg
Phone: +49 (0) 3491-42 91 10, *www.alte-canzley.de*

Luther Hotel ***superior
Neustrassse 7, D-06886 Wittenberg
Phone: +49 (0) 3491-45 80, *www.luther-hotel-wittenberg.de*

Best Western Hotel ****
Collegienstrasse 56/57, D-06886 Wittenberg
Phone: +49 (0) 3491-42 50, *www.bestwestern.de/hotels*

Less expensive and only a six-minute walk from the Castle Church is the family-owned hotel **Am Alten Anker**.
286 Dessauer Strasse, D-06886 Wittenberg
Phone: +49 (0) 3491-76 87 60, *www.amaltenanker.de*

Addresses and Travel Information

Wittenberg Information
Schlossplatz 2, D-06886 Lutherstadt Wittenberg
Phone: +49 (0) 34 91–49 86 10
www.lutherstadt-wittenberg.de,
info@lutherstadt-wittenberg.de

Castle Church (Schlosskirche)
Schlossplatz, 06886 Lutherstadt Wittenberg
Phone: +49 (0)–34 91 40 25 85
www.schlosskirche-wittenberg.de
schlosskirche@kirche-wittenberg.de

Cranach House (Cranachhaus)
Markt 4, D-06886 Lutherstadt Wittenberg
Cranach Courtyard (Cranachhof)
Schlossstrasse 1, 06886 Lutherstadt Wittenberg
Phone: +49 (0) 34 91–420 19 11
www.cranach-stiftung.de
info@cranach-stiftung.de

City Church of St. Mary (Stadtkirche St. Marien)
Bugenhagen House (Bugenhagenhaus)
Kirchplatz, D-06886 Lutherstadt Wittenberg
Phone: +49 (0) 34 91–62 83 0
www.stadtkirchengemeinde-wittenberg.de
stadtkirche@kirche-wittenberg.de

Leucorea University (Stiftung Leucorea)
Collegienstrasse 62, D-06886 Lutherstadt Wittenberg,
Phone: +49 (0) 34 91–46 61 00
https://leucorea.de/

Melanchthon House (Melanchthonhaus)
Collegienstrasse 60, D-06886 Lutherstadt Wittenberg
Phone: +49 (0) 34 91–42 03 11 0
www.martinluther.de
melanchthonhaus@martinluther.de

Luther House (Lutherhaus)

Stiftung Luthergedenkstätten in Sachsen-Anhalt)
Collegienstrasse 54, D-06886 Lutherstadt Wittenberg
Phone: +49 (0) 34 91–42 03 11 8
www.martinluther.de
info@martinluther.de

Organ Concerts in the Castle and City Churches

Castle Church (Ladegast Organ):
May–October, Tues, 2.30 p.m. – 3 p.m.
City Church (Sauer Organ):
May–October, Fridays, 6 p.m. – 6.30 p.m.
May–October in the Castle and City Churches, Sat, 5 p.m.

Medieval Faires

Twice a year, Wittenberg turns into a medieval village, with music, costumes, peasant fare, wine and beer, medieval dancing, juggling and processions, and people from near and far. There is also an annual Pottery Fair in September.

Wittenberg Faires

Luther's Hochzeit is an annual celebration based on the wedding of Luther and Katharina von Bora. The next date is June 9–11, 2017. The ReformationsFest is another Medieval Faire, with classical concerts, plays, seminars and church services taking place for several days around October 31.

Guided City Tours in English

The Tourist Office arranges English tours for groups, but the regular daily tours are in German. A self-guided audio tour in English is available, also accessible by cell phone, for only the connection fee.

ENGLISH SERVICES IN WITTENBERG

The Evangelical Lutheran Church of America invites pilgrims to come to Lutherstadt Wittenberg to explore their faith, their Lutheran identity, and God's mission of healing and reconciliation in the world. In Wittenberg, the English Ministry will offer church services in English between May 1 and October 31, which will alternate between the City Church of St. Mary and the Castle Church, on Saturdays at 5 p.m., and also on Wednesdays, Thursdays, and Fridays at 4 p.m. or 4:30 p.m. in the Corpus Christi Chapel. The services will be conducted by guest pastors, mostly from the United States, but also Canada and Australia. Pastors from these countries can apply for a two-week-stay to give the sermon in Wittenberg, but there is a five-year waiting list. More at:

Rev. Robert Flohrs, WEM Director
Schlossplatz 2, D-06886 Lutherstadt Wittenberg,
info@wittenbergenglishministry.com
www.wittenbergenglishministry.com/

Another opportunity to meet English speakers in Wittenberg is the Thursday evening "Stammtisch" (conversation group) event with local pastors and Germans who want to practice their English (see below for contact information).

The locally run "College Wittenberg" offers inexpensive lodging for up to 48 people as well as seminar rooms, a cafeteria, laundry facilities, bikes, and other amenities.

More at:
www.elca.org/wittenberg
wittenberg@elca.org
Phone in the US:
1 800–638-522
1 773–380-2700
See also:
www.american-churchberlin.de

A statue of Katharina von Bora in the Luther House courtyard. She ran the estate, a former convent, for her husband. He referred to her as "Katie," or "mein Herr Käthe," my husband Kate.

Chapter Three
Luther's Allies
The Wittenberg Community, from Katharina to Cranach

Katharina von Bora was Luther's wife and soulmate. In 1531, he praised her virtues. "I would not trade my Katie for both France and Venice," he wrote. "First, because God gave her to me, and He gave me to her; second, because I often notice that other women have more faults than she does (though she has a few of her own, she has many great virtues offsetting them); third, because she keeps the fides matrimonii, that is, the faith and honor of marriage."

Katharina von Bora

Luther had always been critical of celibacy and monastic vows. Even before the Reformation, monks and nuns left their monasteries to get married. Luther supported them. Yet his 1525 wedding to Katharina von Bora was a surprise.

On April 7, 1523, twelve nuns hidden in herring barrels escaped from the abbey at Nimbschen, near Grimma. Nine of them came to Wittenberg. Luther organised places for them to stay. His efforts were successful for eight of them, but he was unable to find a place for the ninth—a nun named Katharina von Bora—because she kept turning down offers. Finally, she suggested that she and Luther should marry. In 1524, the Peasants' War against the aristocracy had broken out, in which hundreds of thousands of peasants were killed, but priests as well. Luther intended his marriage to be a sign of faith in God during the war. He wanted to "practice what he had been preaching" about the objectionable nature of celibacy.

His friend Philipp Melanchthon believed the timing of the wedding to be disastrous, because the Peasants' War required Luther's authority. And contemporaries were floating a legend that a marriage between a monk and a nun would beget the Antichrist. However, the illustrations of Luther's *New Testament* and his "Against the Execrable Bull of the Antichrist" made it clear whom Luther saw as the Antichrist: the author of the bull excommunicating him from the Church. Needless to say, Katharina shared this view.

Katharina von Bora came from a noble family that had hit on hard times. But thanks to her years in the abbey, she had received an education that surpassed that of most other women of her era. Luther allowed her to retain her maiden name, which kept the memory of her noble ancestry alive.

When Luther got married, Frederick the Wise gave him the salary of a professor as well as the Augustinian Monastery to live in. To be sure, the condition of the building was deplorable. Luther's straw bed had not been aired out properly by his negligent servant, so it was moldy. But Katharina managed to turn the monastery into the flourishing Luther House. To supplement the family income, she turned some of the rooms into student housing. Before long, Martin Luther, Katharina, and their six children became symbols for a new middle-class Christianity and a role model for other pastors' families.

The way Luther addressed Katharina in his letters documents how much he loved her. In his will, he named her as his heiress—quite unusual then. Much to her dismay, however, Saxony Chancellor Gregor Brück would not allow it. Katharina von Bora died in 1552 in Torgau (page 165).

LUTHER'S CHILDREN

Luther and Katharina had six children together—Johannes, Elisabeth, Magdalena, Martin, Paul, and Margarete (picture right). Luther cared a lot about his children. He sent them letters, gave them presents, and often described them as his greatest joy. His children were privately tutored by his students. He was particularly strict with his oldest son, Hans, born on June 7, 1526. His unreasonably high expectations inevitably led to disappointments. Enrolled at the university at age seven in 1533, Hans completed the bachelor's degree exam in 1539.

Hans was sent to a good school in Torgau, with his cousin Florian von Bora. He suffered homesickness, but recalling his own school days, Luther insisted that he stick it out. The only time Hans was allowed to return to Wittenberg was when his sister Magdalene became ill. Luther was preparing his daughter for the possibility that God might be calling her to Himself. On September 20, 1542, she died in Luther's arms.

Relatives also resided in the Luther home. Magdalena von Bora, an aunt of Katharina's, who was called "Muhme Lene," stayed with them until her death in 1537. The couple also took in the four children of Luther's deceased sister, two nephews, and a niece of Katharina's. Driven by a deep sense of family, Luther helped select spouses for his nieces and nephews. Occasionally, he took in distant relatives and poor people.

At times, swindlers abused his kindness. In 1541, Luther threw out a "filthy whore," who had wormed her way into the family's trust. She had introduced herself as Rosina von Truchsess, claiming to be an escaped nun. But it turned out she was pregnant and had attempted to abort her child.

Philipp Melanchthon

Philipp Melanchthon came to Wittenberg in May 1518, at age twenty-one. He was born to Georg Schwarzerdt ("black earth" in German), but changed his name to Melanchthon (the Greek rendering of his last name). He had a fast-track career. He enrolled at the University of Heidelberg in 1509, and was a professor in Tübingen from 1514 to 1518. Elector Frederick the Wise turned to the well-known Johannes Reuchlin to fill the teaching position for Greek at the newly founded University of Wittenberg, who recommended his grandnephew, Melanchthon.

Philipp was not taken seriously at first, because upon arriving, the tiny professor, who was just five feet tall, fell off his horse. In his opening lecture on August 29, 1518, however, he won over his audience. Soon, five- to six hundred listeners would crowd into his lecture hall. Melanchthon started to reform the university in accordance with the wishes of Frederick the Wise, which is how he acquired his nickname, *Praeceptor Germaniae*, Teacher of Germany.

In the older Luther, Melanchthon saw the embodiment of true Christian godliness. They became close friends, even though their personalities were entirely different. Melanchthon was timid, insecure, and sensitive, while Luther was outspoken and gruff. Their back doors at Collegienstrasse were connected by an alley, so they could visit each other without being seen from the street. Melanchthon bore the brunt of the responsibility of the "Wittenberg Unrest" during Luther's stay at Wartburg Castle, but once Luther returned, Melanchthon handed the Reformation back to him.

ANDREAS BODENSTEIN VON KARLSTADT

Andreas Rudolph Bodenstein usually went by the name of Karlstadt, after the town in Franconia where he was born in 1486. Karlstadt started out as a friend of Luther, who was fifteen years his junior. He studied in Erfurt and became a professor in Wittenberg. It was he who awarded Luther his doctorate in 1512. When he studied in Rome, the level of corruption within the church shocked him. In 1519, he went to the Leipzig Disputation with Luther (page 143).

While Luther subsequently went into hiding at the Wartburg, Karlstadt took the spiritual lead in Wittenberg. He performed the first Reformed communion service in German on Christmas Day, 1521—until then, it had always been in Latin—in which the congregation did not have to confess before communion and could take both wine and bread.

But soon, he became closer to radical Reformers, such as Huldrych Zwingli and John Calvin. He refused to wear the robe of a priest, conducted services without music, and married a fifteen-year-old girl. In 1524, his followers destroyed church interiors, in the so-called *Bildersturm*. The city called on Luther for help. Karlstadt had to leave Wittenberg and became pastor in Orlamünde, a Thuringian town. Luther took a stand against him in Jena (page 135), and Frederick the Wise expelled him shortly thereafter.

During the Peasants' War, Luther secretly took him in for eight weeks in Wittenberg, on the condition that he recant. In the following years, Karlstadt became a farmer. Eventually, he moved to Switzerland, where he died of the plague in 1541.

GEORG SPALATIN

Georg Spalatin was named after the town of his birth, Spalt (near Nuremberg), where he was born as Johannes Burckhardt on January 17, 1484, but he spent much of his life in Torgau (page 168). He studied at Erfurt and Wittenberg and became part of the court of Electoral Saxony in 1509. Initially working as a librarian, Spalatin advanced to the position of court preacher. He was the intermediary between Luther and Frederick the Wise, evident from more than four hundred letters. Spalatin met Luther early on in Wittenberg, and before he became Luther's "mouthpiece" to the Elector, Spalatin was Luther's theological mentor. A careful and thoughtful man, Spalatin encouraged the Elector to support Luther. After Frederick the Wise died, Spalatin became pastor in Altenburg, where he was able to implement the Reformation. He also was an official delegate at a number of key events: at the Imperial Diet in Speyer in 1526, in Augsburg in 1530, and in Schmalkalden in 1537.

JOHANN VON STAUPITZ

Born in 1468, Johann von Staupitz was an Augustinian hermit, Luther's pastor and mentor, and a staunch defender of the Reformation. After studies in Cologne and Leipzig, he joined the Augustinian Monastery in Munich. He began theology studies in Tübingen in 1497, while serving as prior of the monastery. Frederick, the Elector of Saxony who had known Staupitz from his youth, called him to Wittenberg to help build the university in 1502. In Tübingen, Staupitz had experienced a close relationship between a mendicant order and a university. He applied this model to Wittenberg, where he became professor of Scripture and also the first dean of the theological faculty in 1502. When he left his post in 1512, he was succeeded by Luther. During Luther's years as a monk, Staupitz was his pastor and consoled him in his struggles of conscience.

JOHANNES BUGENHAGEN

Wittenberg-based theologian Johannes Bugenhagen, who came from the Duchy of Pomerania, joined the Reformers in 1520, after studying Luther's writings. He enrolled at the Leucorea in 1521, and with Luther's recommendation, he took the position of Wittenberg's main pastor at the City Church of St. Mary and became Luther's pastor and spiritual caretaker. Bugenhagen and Luther were close friends and collaborators. Bugenhagen performed Luther and Katharina's wedding, baptized their first child, and gave the sermon at Luther's funeral. Bugenhagen also assisted Luther in translating the Bible. His biblical commentaries were very influential.

ELECTOR FREDERICK THE WISE

Frederick III, known as Frederick the Wise, was the man who shielded and protected Luther. In 1486, he became the Elector of Saxony at age twenty-three, governing with his brother John the Steadfast. He represented the Ernestine branch of the House of Wettin, which resided in the city of Torgau (page 165) while the Albertine branch resided in Dresden (page 161). Frederick commissioned many of the best artists. He never married, but he and his mistress Anna Weller von Molsdorf had three children.

Frederick was a devout Catholic, who even went on a pilgrimage to the Holy Land. Yet, he became the leading Saxon prince to back Luther and to demand reform from Holy Roman Emperor Maximilian I. It was part power play against Rome, but he also wanted to modernize the Church. The fact that the Pope had twice refused to let him marry Margaret, daughter of Maximilian I of Habsburg, also factored in. Politically, he was lucky. The ecclesiastical region of Saxony belonged to several bishoprics, namely Meissen, Naumburg, Mainz, Halberstadt, Magdeburg, Brandenburg, Bamberg, and Würzburg. They could not agree on a variety of issues, which strengthened him.

However, he and Luther never met face-to-face, he always depended on Spalatin. Whenever the Elector was asked why he let Luther remain in his territory, he would say, "I do not know anything bad about him. I have nothing to do with him. If he does anything wrong, then discuss the matter with him in Wittenberg where I have a university."

JOHN FREDERICK I THE MAGNANIMOUS

John Frederick I, Elector of Saxony beginning in 1532, was the son of John the Steadfast and the nephew of Frederick the Wise. He was educated by Georg Spalatin, the intermediary between Luther and Frederick the Wise. John Frederick was a devout Protestant, who took a bolder stand against the Pope than his uncle. For instance, he pushed out the Catholic Bishop of Naumburg, Julius von Pflug (page 159).

He became the head of the Schmalkaldic League (*Schmalkaldischer Bund*), a military alliance of Protestant princes against Emperor Charles V, who represented Catholicism—named after the Thuringian town where it was founded (page 129). Luther supplied the theological groundwork for the League. John Frederick's closest ally was Philipp I, Landgrave of Hessen, who resided in Kassel.

In 1546, shortly after Luther's death, the Schmalkaldic War broke out. The Schmalkaldic League was defeated by Imperial troops at the Battle of Mühlberg, mostly because John's younger cousin Maurice of Saxony sided with Charles V. In 1547, John was captured and imprisoned, while the Emperor besieged Wittenberg. John ceded Wittenberg to the Emperor, sparing not only his life, but also his family's, and prevented the city from being destroyed. After that, he was called the Magnanimous. He also moved the Wittenberg library to Jena (page 135). Maurice of Saxony became the new Elector. John was released after five years and took residence in Weimar, where he died in 1554.

Lucas Cranach the Elder

Lucas Cranach the Elder was one of the most influential painters of the Late Middle Ages, at a time when paintings and illustrations were full of meaning, because few people could read and write. He was a court painter to Lutheran princes, including Frederick the Wise and John Frederick I. When people think of Luther today, they visualize Cranach's paintings, the first of which dates to 1520. In December 1521, Luther traveled in disguise from Wartburg Castle to Wittenberg and Cranach made the woodcut of *"Junker Jörg."*

One of their greatest joint ventures was printing the New Testament in German, published just before September 25, 1522. It included twenty-one full-page woodcuts by Cranach. The five thousand copies sold out quickly and a second edition followed three months later. By 1534, seventeen printings had been done in Wittenberg alone. Each copy cost ten and a half groschen, whereas the bound form probably cost one guilder (the price of a pig ready for slaughter).

Cranach became one of the richest men in town. He owned multiple homes, a license for a pharmacy, one to sell wine in taverns, and a bookstore, located at Marktplatz 3. He also served on Wittenberg's city council and as a mayor. Luther was the godfather of Cranach's youngest daughter.

One of Cranach's famous paintings is *The Ten Commandments*, now exhibited in the Luther House. A Cranach painting known as the *Reformation Altar* is displayed in the City Church and is notable because it was dedicated during the Schmalkaldic War on April 24, 1547, the day John Frederick I was defeated. It depicts the Lord's Supper. The servant handing the chalice to Luther is his son, Lucas Cranach the Younger. Luther is portrayed as Junker Jörg from the Wartburg. Another of Cranach's paintings displayed in the City Church is the epitaph for Paulus Eber, a professor of theology, depicting a vineyard, the biblical metaphor for the Church. Cranach shows the Pope as destroying the vineyard, with monks and cardinals ripping out vines while the Reformers take care of them. Luther is pulling weeds; Melanchthon is drawing clear water; and Bugenhagen is raking the ground.

Cranach painted the wedding portrait of Luther and Katharina. His last Luther picture is from 1539. At age fifty-six, the Reformer is portrayed as heavyset, meant to symbolize Lutheran stability and confidence. Cranach followed John Frederick I into captivity in 1550, and to Weimar in 1552, where he died one year later at age seventy-one (page 139).

LUTHER ROSE – THE SEAL OF LUTHER

This is how Luther described his seal on July 8, 1530, "First, we have a black cross lying on a heart. This reminds me that it is only faith in the Crucified One that saves us. ... Although that cross is black—that is, even though it kills and is supposed to hurt—the  heart retains its natural color. This means that the cross does not destroy the heart's nature. In other words, the cross does not kill, but keeps alive. This heart is at the center of a white rose. This shows that faith gives joy, consolation, and peace. ... The rose should be white and not red, because white is the color of the spirits and all angels. This rose is in a sky-blue field because joy in spirit and faith is the beginning of the future. ... And place a gold ring in that field [as a sign] that this blessedness is eternal in heaven and that it is more precious than all joy and possessions, just as gold is the highest, most precious metal."

Luther and the Jews

Luther's attitude toward the Jews changed over the years. In 1523, he published the text, *That Jesus Christ Was Born a Jew,* trying to evangelize them. At that point in his ministry, he was against anyone who discriminated against Jews. Yet by the end of his life, Luther was disappointed that his attempts to attract Jews to the Gospel were unsuccessful, so he wrote books against them. Case in point, he sarcastically describes the sculpture on the City Church (Stadtkirche) at Wittenberg:

> "Here in Wittenberg there is a pig carved in stone on our parish church. Under it are young piglets and Jews who are suckling. Behind the pig stands a rabbi, who is lifting up the pig's right leg and pulling its rear over himself with his left hand. Stooping over, he is diligently looking at the pig from under its rear, peering into the Talmud, as though intending to read and discover some subtle and special detail."

His 1543 text, *On the Jews and Their Lies*, calls for burning down synagogues and banishing Jews who do not want to work from the cities—following the example of France, Spain, and Bohemia.

While Bertolt Brecht considers critique of Luther on these issues to be legitimate, he does arrive at the fair conclusion that "Luther's hostility toward the Jews should not be interpreted as psychological or as pathologically hate-filled. It is not political, nor an extension of governmental anti-Judaism. Rather, Luther's…conflict with the Jews was essentially religious and theological." Centuries later, the National Socialists would use Luther's theologically motivated hostility toward Jews for their racially motivated anti-Semitism.

The following 1543 mandate on Jews in Saxony explicitly ascribes the ethical faults of Jews to their "bloodline" and in that respect cannot be credited to Luther. The mandate demands:

> "First, their synagogues or schools should be set on fire, and whatever does not burn should be piled up and covered so that no one may see a stone or ashes from it forever, and such should be done to the glory of our Lord and Christianity. In this way, God will see that we are Christians and

have not knowingly endured or condoned such public lies, curses, and blasphemies of His Son and our Christ…

"Moses writes that when a city practices idolatry, it should be completely destroyed with fire, and nothing should be left remaining of it. If he were alive today, he would be the first to set the Jewish schools and houses on fire….As they have clearly persecuted us Christians around the world from the very beginning, and still would gladly do so if they were able, Jews have often also tried to and were forcefully struck on the snout for it. From childhood on, they have imbibed such bitter hatred toward the Goiim [Gentiles] from their parents and rabbis, and they continuously imbibe hate into themselves so that it runs through the blood and flesh, through the marrow and bones, and has become their nature and way of life—through and through…

"Therefore, dear Christian, know this and do not doubt that—with the exception of the devil—you have no more bitter, venomous, and fierce enemy than a true Jew who earnestly intends to be a Jew. There may well be those among them who believe what the cattle and geese believe; nevertheless, the bloodline adheres to them all. Hence, they are often blamed in historical accounts for poisoning wells and stealing and impaling children…"

LUTHER AND THE TURKS

Luther was no friend of the Turks, either, In the sixteenth century, the Turks posed a tremendous challenge to the Christian West, since this Islamic superpower had control over the Near East, North Africa, and the Balkans. In 1526, they defeated the Hungarian army, and in 1529, they stood at the gates of Vienna, though they were fought off.

This was much on Luther's mind, and he even referred to the Turkish war in Thesis Five (of the 95 Theses). In his text, *On War Against the Turk*, he rejected the latter's right to attack other countries. He was able to refer to the Qur'an in his polemics, since he was familiar with the Latin version.

The Luther Fountain in Luther Square was constructed in 1913 by Paul Juckoff. It depicts Luther as a thirteen-year-old boy on his way into the world. On top of the stele is St. George, the dragonslayer, the patron saint of Mansfeld.

Chapter Four
Luther's Roots
Growing up in Mansfeld: A Tough Life Among Miners

Not much is known about Martin Luther's childhood and early life. He was born on November 10, 1483, in Eisleben, as the second son of a copper mine owner named Hans Luder, and his wife Margarethe. In its heyday, Eisleben was surrounded by copper mines and quite wealthy.

In Luther's time, Eisleben and all of the surrounding area was governed by the counts of Mansfeld. After World War II, the area became part of Communist East Germany; Eisleben still has a veteran's cemetary dedicated to the soldiers of the Red Army. Now, after reunification, it is in the State of Saxony-Anhalt, but is no longer the county seat.

Only one day after his birth, Luther was baptized in the Church of Saints Peter and Paul in Eisleben. The baby was named after the saint of the day: Martin.

Luther's father came from a farm in the Thuringian town of Möhra, but he had to leave because his oldest brother inherited the farm, as was customary in that part of Germany (or he could have stayed and become a field hand working for his brother). In 1484, Hans Luder moved his small family to Mansfeld near Eisleben, then an up-and-coming mining town surrounded by a city wall, with its own city hall, library, and many prosperous buildings. The Luder/Luther family had many relatives in the wider neighborhood. Even today, "Luther" is one of the most common last names in the region. Hans Luder started as a common miner, worked his way up, and eventually made his career as a copper mine owner, when he leased a mine from the counts of Mansfeld. Some books say he even became an alderman in the City Council.

From 1488, at the age of four and a half, until 1496, Martin Luther was enrolled at the Trivialschule, the elementary school in Mansfeld. School was taught in Latin, as was customary then. So Luther learned Latin early on and could already speak it as a child. He also learned to read, write, and do mathematics. Young Martin's education was marked by thriftiness and strictness, also quite common then. His memories of school were not very pleasant, since beatings with a rod and other punishments were the daily standard.

He was also beaten by his parents when he did not obey—one of the reasons he left home early for higher education. But because his father was what would be considered middle class today, at least young Luther did not have to work and was permitted to get an education.

The school building was destroyed by a fire between 1570 and 1575. A new edifice was built in its place. For centuries, a building on Lutherstrasse 8, the site of the principal's office, was mistaken for Luther's school. When a city chronicle written by Cyriacus Spangenberg in 1553–1574 was discovered, however, the mistake was revealed. The edifice on the historic school grounds was taken down in 2000, due to dilapidation. A new building similar to the original Luther school was erected, which now serves as a tourist information office.

Commenting on his family background and ancestors, Martin Luther wrote:

> "I am the son of a peasant. My great-grandfather, grandfather, and father were truly peasants. But my father insisted I should become a director, a mayor or whatever else they have in the village—a chief servant, rising above the others. Later, my father moved to Mansfeld and became a miner. That is where I am from."

Even today one can see the hills created by copper mining surrounding Mansfeld and Eisleben. The mines were all closed just a few years ago, though, due to depletion.

SIGHTS IN MANSFELD

Luther's Home Church, the Church of St. George

This church was built in the Late Gothic style between 1497 and 1518. As a boy, Luther served as an acolyte in the sanctuary, which was constructed in the Romanesque period and is partly preserved. In addition to a painting of the resurrection by Lucas Cranach, this church also boasts the only full-length portrait of Luther painted in Cranach's workshop.

Home of Luther's Parents

In 1483–84, Luther's parents moved from Eisleben to Mansfeld, where they rented a house at Spangenbergstrasse 2. It has been rebuilt since; the door with the arch at the back of the building is the only part still remaining from that historic era.

Luther's Elementary School (Lutherschule)

This building is more or less a replica of Luther's school. The original building burnt down before the Thirty Years' War. Today, the tourist information resides here. There are still original parts in the basement.

Addresses and Travel Information

Mansfeld City Information (Stadtinformation Mansfeld) (former Luther Elementary School)
Junghuhnstrasse 2, D-06343 Mansfeld-Lutherstadt
Phone: +49 (0) 34782–9 03 42
www.mansfeld.eu, stadtinfo@mansfeld.eu

Church of St. George (St. Georgs-Kirche)
Lutherstrasse 7, D-06343 Mansfeld-Lutherstadt
Phone: +49 (0) 34782–909 929
www.lutherstaedte-eisleben-mansfeld.de
mansfeld-evangelisch@gmx.de

The House of Luther's Parents (Luthers Elternhaus)
Lutherstrasse 26, D-06343 Mansfeld-Lutherstadt
Phone: +49 (0) 34782–919 38 10
www.martinluther.de, elternhaus@martinluther.de

Mansfeld Castle (Schloss Mansfeld)
Schloss Mansfeld 1, D-06343 Mansfeld-Lutherstadt
Phone: +49 (0) 34782–2 02 01
www.schloss-mansfeld.de, info@schloss-mansfeld.de

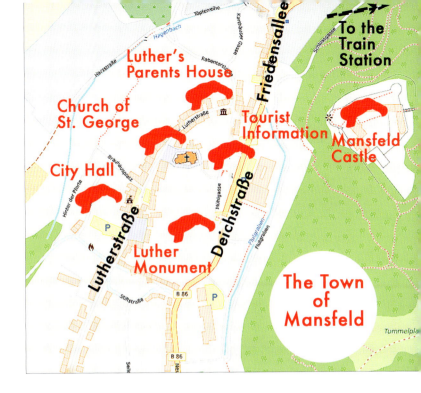

HOW TO GET TO MANSFELD AND EISLEBEN

Eisleben is connected by regional train, once an hour in the daytime. It is half an hour to Halle, and about one hour and 15 to 30 minutes to Erfurt, Leipzig, or Magdeburg. Mansfeld, a few miles northwest of Eisleben, does not have a train, but the bus No 420 to Mansfeld leaves from Eisleben hourly at various locations, including the train station and Breiter Weg.

From Eisleben to Mansfeld, it is 30 to 40 minutes by bus, and 15 minutes by car. Both towns are about 20 miles off Autobahn A 9 from Berlin to Nuremberg (and Munich).

Picture left: The Mansfeld Castle, documented since 1229, was the ancestral seat of the Counts of Mansfeld. Luther traveled here shortly before his death to mediate their struggle. Today, the castle is an (affordable) guest house for Christian Youth groups. It has 26 renovated rooms for 80 people (www.schloss-mansfeld.de/unser-haus).

The Luther Monument in Eisleben, the city where Luther was born, and where he died. It was designed by Rudolf Siemering in 1883. In the background is the Church of St. Andrew on the Market Square.

Birth And Death in Eisleben

Luther was on good terms with the counts of Mansfeld. In 1546, the counts had a falling out with each other over an issue relatd to mining. Luther was asked to come and mediate. The meeting was scheduled to take place in Eisleben.

The journey was hazardous, and Katharina was greatly concerned about her husband. The negotiations lasted until February 17, when Luther was too weak to participate. He had dinner with his companions, went to his room and said his evening prayer at eight o clock. Shortly thereafter he was plagued by pains, particularly chest pains, which probably were caused by angina pectoris. Aurifaber, one of his companions, went to the counts to obtain some medication made from the shaving of a unicorn. Afterward, Luther was able to sleep again, but he woke up at one o'clock in the morning with more pain, expecting he might well die in the city of his birth. He confidently prayed Psalm 68:20, "Our god is a God of salvation and to God the Lord belong deliverances from death."

One of Luther's last prayers has been handed down. It is revealing his life with God, in light of the Gospel that he discovered. In 1566, his friend and first biographer Johannes Matthesius described the end of Luther's life and his last prayer:

"Oh my heavenly Father, God and Father of our Lord Jesus Christ, God of all comfort, I thank You that You have revealed to me Your dear son, Jesus Christ, in whom I believe, whom I have preached and confessed, whom I have loved and praised, whom the wretched Pope and all godless dishonor, persecute, and blaspheme.…

"I ask You, my Lord Jesus: let my soul be commended into Your hands. O heavenly Father, even though I am leaving this body and being torn away from this life, I still know for certain that I will remain with You forever and that no one can tear me out of Your hands…"

When all kinds of medicine were pushed on him, he said once more, "I am going away," and, "Into Your hands I commit my spirit; You have redeemed me, O Lord, faithful God," three times in quick succession. Then he became quiet.

His friends called to him, but he shut his eyes. They asked him whether he wished to die and he answered clearly, "Yes."

For Elector John Frederick I, the death of his protégé was a great loss. He arranged for the Reformer's body to be returned to Wittenberg and buried in the Castle Church.

Luther was wrapped in a white gown and transported in a pewter casket to the nearby Church of St. Andrew. On February 19, Justus Jonas preached Luther's funeral sermon. The body was carried from the city toward Halle, where it was kept overnight in the sacristy of the Church of St. Mary. The next day the procession reached Bitterfeld, Saxony.

On February 22, his burial took place in Wittenberg, with Bugenhagen preaching the sermon and Melanchthon giving a memorial speech by the casket. The location of the tomb was chosen with great care—under the pulpit—because it was Luther's most important place of work.

In his memorial speech, Melanchthon said: "Those who knew him did not know what magnificent humanity he possessed, how friendly he was in his personal exchanges with others, how rarely he was quarrelsome or cantankerous! And yet everything was related to the zeal that is fitting for such a man.…Hence it is clear that his harshness elsewhere flowed out of zeal for the truth, not out of quarrelsomeness and bitterness. To that, we and many who are not present are all witnesses."

Hotels in Eisleben

Hotel Graf von Mansfeld & Restaurant ***
Markt 56, D-06295 Eisleben
Phone: +49 (0) 3475–66 300 *www.hotel-eisleben.de*

Deckert's Hotel am Katharinenstift ***
Sangerhäuser Str. 12, D-06295 Eisleben
Phone: +49 (0) 3475–63 26 70
www.deckerts-hotel.de

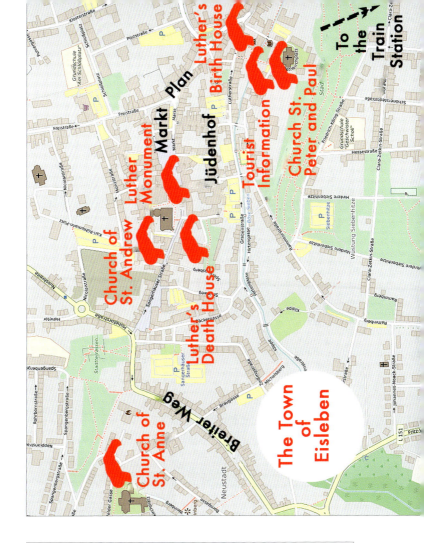

Hotels in Eisleben

Hotel Mansfelder Hof ***
Hallesche Str. 33, D-06295 Eisleben
Phone: +49 (0) 3475–61 26 20; *www.mansfelderhof.de*

Hotel Alter Simpel
Glockenstrasse 7, D-06295 Eisleben
Phone: +49 (0) 3475–696507
www.hotelaltersimpel-eisleben.de/

SIGHTS IN EISLEBEN

Luther's Birth House (Luthers Geburtshaus)

Luther's birth house was built on Petristrasse in the middle of the 15th century. It is now a museum. Martin Luther was born there on November 10, 1493. As early as 1693, the city renovated the home as a memorial for Luther and the Reformation, making it one of the oldest museums in the German-speaking world. In 1817, Luther School (Lutherschule) was built on the neighboring property for the 300th anniversary of the Reformation.

Church of Saints Peter and Paul (St. Petri Pauli)

This hall church with three naves is where Luther was baptized on November 11, 1483. The foundation for the present building was laid in 1486, but the mighty church steeple had already been erected. Its spire was remodeled in 1566, when it received the roof hood. Since the 16th century, the interior has changed several times. In the choir vault is a piece of the original painting of 1904–05. In 2011, the interior was renovated. Along with artworks like the medieval St. Anna altar, the crucifix, and Luther's reconstructed baptismal font, there is also a modern baptismal font.

Church of St. Andrew (Andreaskirche)

Martin Luther gave his last sermon in this church. Most of this Late Gothic hall church was constructed in the 15th century. The baroque domes of the "watchman's towers" (*Hausmannstürme*) date to the year 1601. Virtually no changes have been made to the pulpit since Luther's days. The tombs of the counts who ruled in the county of Mansfeld are in the aisles. The busts of Martin Luther and Philipp Melanchthon, also in the church, were made by the great Prussian sculptor Johann Gottfried Schadow.

Martin Luther held his last sermon from the historic pulpit in the Church of St. Andrew, on February 15, 1546, only a few days before he died. The pulpit was in severe disrepair for quite some time, but it has been restored.

The Minneapolis Institute of Art in Minnesota, the largest art museum in the United States outside of New York, donated the money necessary for restoring it. The cost for reconstruction was about $70,000. In return, the historic pulpit will be displayed in the Minnesota museum as the centerpiece of the exhibition, "Here I Stand. Martin Luther: Art and the Reformation," taking place up to the 2017 Luther Year. More at:

new.artsmia.org/luther

Church of St. Anne (St. Annen-Kirche)

The cornerstone for the miners' Church of St. Anne was laid in 1514. The Augustinian Hermits' monastery (founded in 1515), was deeply affiliated with the church. Serving as district vicar of the Augustinian order, Luther visited this first Lutheran church in the area several times. The "Eisleben Stone Picture Bible" (*Eisleben Steinbilder-Bibel*), fashioned by Hans Thon Uttendrup from Münster in 1585, is noteworthy, consisting of twenty-nine sandstone slabs in relief, depicting important scenes from the Old Testament.

Luther's Death House (Luthers Sterbehaus)

The house were Luther died is at Andreaskirchplatz, right across from the Church of St. Andrew. It was built for the town clerk in 1498, after a fire that destroyed much of Eisleben. The house is landmarked and now serves as a Luther museum. It was renovated completely in recent years and reopened in February 2013. Exhibits include the bed in which Luther died and many other historic artifacts, including a kitchen.

Addresses and Travel Information

Tourist-Information
Lutherstadt Eisleben & Stadt Mansfeld e.V.
Hallesche Strasse 4-6, D-06295 Lutherstadt Eisleben
Phone: +49 (0) 3475–60 21 24
www.lutherstaedte-eisleben-mansfeld.de
info@lutherstaedte-eisleben-mansfeld.de

Luther's Birth House (Luthers Geburtshaus)
(Stiftung Luthergedenkstiitten)
Lutherstrasse 15, D-06295 Lutherstadt Eisleben
Phone: +49 (0) 3475–71 47 81 4
www.martinluther.de, geburtshaus@martinluther.de

Church of Peter and Paul (St. Petri Pauli)
Petrikirchplatz, D-06295 Lutherstadt Eisleben
Phone: +49 (0) 3475–711 80 22
www.kirche-in-eisleben.de/english.html

Church of St. Andrew (St. Andreas)
Andreaskirchplatz 11, D-06295 Lutherstadt Eisleben
Phone: +49 (0) 3475–60 22 29
www.kirche-in-eisleben.de/english.html
Organ Concerts: May 1–Sept. 30, Tuesdays, 12–12:30 p.m.

Church of St. Anne (St. Annen)
Annenkirchplatz 2, D-06295 Lutherstadt Eisleben
Phone: +49 (0) 3475–60 41 15
www.kirche-eisleben-stannen.de, st.annen-eisleben@freenet.de
Open after the worship service around 11 a.m at most Sunday, except during the summer

Luther's Death House (Luthers Sterbehaus)
Andreaskirchplatz 7, D-06295 Lutherstadt Eisleben
Phone: +49 (0) 3475–71 47 84 0
www.martinluther.de, sterbehaus@martinluther.de

The Magdeburg Cathedral at night. During the Thirty Years' War, when the city was nearly annihilated, a few thousand people managed to survive by hiding here. The Cathedral is so tall that it can be seen from afar.

School in Magdeburg

At age fourteen, Luther transferred to the school of the Brethen of the Common Life in Magdeburg. The Brethen were a Roman Catholic pietist community founded in the Netherlands, who preached the simple life. His friend Hans Reinicke accompanied Luther to Magdeburg; the boy lived there in the home of Dr. Paul Mosshauer, a representative of the archbishop at clerical proceedings. Mosshauer was from Mansfeld and had relatives there who became masters in the trade of mining. It is very likely that Mosshauer recommended that Luther attend school in Magdeburg. After one year, at age fifteen, Luther transferred to the Latin School of St. George in Eisenach.

Luther did not leave many traces in Magdeburg, and his city is long gone. Then one of the largest and wealthiest cities in Germany that also became a Lutheran stronghold, Magdeburg was nearly wiped out during the Thirty Years' War over the power of the Holy Roman Empire of the German Nation, in which the Habsburg-Catholic monarchies of Austria, Poland, and Spain fought against France and the Protestant alliance uniting the Netherlands, Denmark, and Sweden. In the fragmented German states, one third of the population died.

Magdeburg was conquered by imperial troops. 30,000 citizens were killed—nearly the whole population. Although houses of God were also burned down, about 4,000 Magdeburgers found refuge in the cathedral for three days. When the victors forced the doors open, cathedral preacher Reinhard Bake flung himself at commander Johann Tilly's feet and begged for mercy. The general spared the survivors.

Only about 450 survivors dared to make a fresh start. They built a new, second city over the ruins. However, in World War II on January 16, 1945, most of the city was destroyed by British bombers, including the cathedral. It would be decades before the cathedral was restored.

Magdeburg's Blood Wedding

The "Blood Wedding" in Magdeburg on May 10, 1631 (Julian calendar), was the bloodiest massacre of the Thirty Years' War. The term "wedding" was intended to describe the forced union between the emperor and the virgin on Magdeburg's town crest. In actuality, however, imperial Catholic troops commanded by Johann Tilly completely destroyed the city. How did it come to the bloodbath that stunned Europe? What sealed the fate of the Hanseatic city?

Magdeburg's strategic location and wealth caught the attention of the warring parties, thanks to the miserable Börde region surrounding it. The city had also refused to make payments to the emperor for over a hundred years. Magdeburgers were stubborn and proud, and had become early followers of Martin Luther's teachings. For a long time, the city council tried to remain neutral, but Emperor Ferdinand II, originally from Bohemia-Austria, tried to enforce a re-Catholicization policy that put Magdeburg under increasing pressure. The city was first besieged by imperial troops under General Albrecht von Wallenstein in 1629, who withdrew when the Hanseatic League intervened. A new city council in Magdeburg sought to collaborate with the Protestant camp, and formed an alliance with Swedish King Gustavus Adolphus.

Then Wallenstein's successor Tilly advanced about 22,000 soldiers to the city wall, where his representative Gottfried Heinrich zu Pappenheim had already begun the siege with a troop of 6,000 men and was urgently awaiting reinforcements. During the previous year, Swedish commander Colonel Dietrich von Falkenberg had commissioned fortifications to better protect the city. But the Magdeburg population was divided: a Catholic minority within the upper class longed for the arrival of the imperial troops, and among the Protestants there were hawks and doves. Instead of surrendering to the superior imperial troops, which would have saved the city—because Magdeburg, meanwhile, was running out of gun powder—many pinned their hope on the arrival of the Swedish troops.

But Tilly's army was also short on supplies. As soldiers deserted and horses died, Tilly saw the approaching Swedes as a threat. In April 1631, Gustavus Adolphus had conquered Frankfurt on the Oder and was marching across Brandenburg on his way to Magdeburg. Fearing the Swedes, Emperor Ferdinand had already ordered his generals to withdraw, to block Gustavus Adolfphus's path to the south. The besiegers attacked one last time with the battle cry "Jesus Maria," taking the Magdeburgers by surprise. Half of the sentries had left their posts on the wall, to "enjoy some sweet slumber—but what a costly sleep and atrocious awakening," Friedrich Schiller wrote in his *History of the Thirty Years' War.*

The imperial troops succeeded in infiltrating the city, where a bitter battle raged from house to house. Fires reduced entire streets to ash and rubble. Victory unleashed a bloodlust in the emaciated mercenaries, which ended in a staggering excess of violence. Otto von Guericke, who became mayor in 1646, summed up the destruction, "There was nothing but murder, arson, looting, torment, and bludgeoning." The imperial troops "left a river red with blood, in which clusters of charred bodies floated, streets strewn with corpses." All of Europe was appalled. Even Generals Tilly and Pappenheim were shocked. They could have used a rich, vibrant city as a military outpost in Northern Germany, but now Magdeburg lay in ruins, in which life was hardly feasible, even for soldiers.

Historians still argue today about the cause of the fires. Did Pappenheim have them set to create chaos? Or was it Dietrich von Falkenburg himself, destroying Tilly's prize at his moment of victory?

Right: The Foolish Virgins at the Cathredral, a sculpture from 1250.

Sights in Magdeburg

Church of St. John, Luther Monument

The foundation of this church was laid between 936 and 941. It was first documented in 941, when it was mentioned as a parish church given to the Abbey of St. Maurice by King Otto. Luther preached here in 1524, on the topic of true and false justice. The Reformer's sermon made such a huge impression on his listeners that the city became Lutheran. Emil Hundrieser designed a Luther Monument in 1886, commemorating the sermon. The statue's original pedestal was replaced by a concrete foundation in 1966. On May 29, 1995, the original pedestal was put in place again, along with the inscription, "God's word with us eternally."

Walloon Church (Wallonerkirche)

This church was founded in 1285, by monks of the Augustinian Monastery. Jubilee indulgences were celebrated in 1396, and because Magdeburg was appointed as the only place to offer such pardons within a sixty-kilometer (approximately forty-mile) radius, it drew many pilgrims. Luther visited this church and its Augustinian monks in 1516, spending the night in one of the monastery's dormitories.

In 1524, he returned for another visit and preached there. That same year, the abbot dissolved the monastery and handed over its facilities to the city of Magdeburg. From then on, the church was used only for secular purposes. After the Thirty Years' War, it was no longer maintained, nor used after 1639.

In 1690, by order of Elector Frederick William, Lutheran Walloon refugees got the church, and since then it has been known as the Walloon Church.

The Magdeburg Cathedral (Magdeburger Dom)

As early as 955 AD—even before being crowned Emperor—Otto I began building a cathedral in Magdeburg, in the Ottonian Romanesque style. It was the predecessor of the modern-day cathedral and beautifully adorned. In 1207, a fire destroyed the cathedral and most of the city of Magdeburg. Years later, a new cathedral was constructed next to the old one, using the original rocks and pillars. The Reformation had an impact on the cathedral: after being shuttered for twenty years, it was reopened and became Lutheran in 1567—celebrating its first Lutheran church service on the first Sunday of Advent that year.

Addresses and Travel Information

Tourist Information Magdeburg
Breiter Weg 22, D-39104 Magdeburg
Phone: +49 (0) 63–60 14 02, *www.magdeburg-tourist.de*

Church of St. John with Luther Monument
Johannisbergstrasse 1, D-39104 Magdeburg
Phone: +49 (0) 391–59 34 45 0
www.mvgm.de/de/johanniskirche/

The Walloon Church
Wallonerberg, D-39104 Magdeburg
Phone: +49 (0) 391–59 75 10 80, *www.ekmd-reformiert.de*

The Magdeburg Cathedral
Am Dom 1, D-39104 Magdeburg
Phone: +49 (0) 3 91–54 10 43 6, *www.magdeburgerdom.de*

Hotels in Magdeburg

Hotel Maritim ****
Otto-von-Guericke-Strasse 87. D-39104 Magdeburg
Phone: +49 (0) 391–59 49 0
www.maritim.de, info.mag@maritim.de

Hotel Herrenkrug ****
Herrenkrug 3, D-39114 Magdeburg
Phone: +49 (0) 391–8 50 80
www.herrenkrug.de, info@herrenkrug.de

Parkhotel Best Western ****
Goethestrasse 38, D-39108 Magdeburg
Phone: +49 (0) 391–7 38 03
www.geheimer-rat.bestwestern.de

Motel One ***
Domplatz 5, D-39104 Magdeburg
Phone: +49 (0) 391–555 5450
magdeburg@motel-one.com

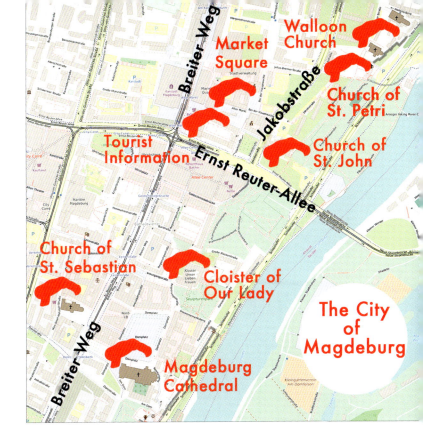

Hotels in Magdeburg

Hotel Ratswaage ****
Ratswaageplatz 1–4. D-39104 Magdeburg
Phone: +49 (0) 391–5 92 60
www.ratswaage.de, hotel@ratswaage.de

Plaza Hotel Magdeburg ****
Halberstädter Strasse 146–150, D-39112 Magdeburg
Phone: +49 (0) 391–6 05 10
www.plazahotelmagdeburg.de

Ramada Magdeburg ****
Hansapark 2, 39116 D-Magdeburg
Phone: +49 (0) 391–6 36 30
www.ramada.de/magdeburg, magdeburg@ramada.de

Coswig is the first stop on the Lutherweg *in Saxony-Anhalt. This is the church of Klieken, a suburb of Coswig. It is famous for its altarpieces by Lucas Cranach the Elder, depicting the Virgin Mary and the Child Jesus.*

Luther Trail in Saxony-Anhalt

Those who don't want to miss any church, house, or castle, in which Luther set foot, can now walk the Luther Trail (Lutherweg), a project created by Protestant churches, tourism organizations, and cities. As of October 2016, five trails on the path of Martin Luther have been designated, in five German states—Saxony-Anhalt, Saxony, Thuringia, Frankonia, and Hessen—with more than one hundred towns altogether. It is one of many endavours to celebrate the 500th anniversary of the Reformation. The *Lutherweg* has twenty-seven stops in Saxony-Anhalt alone—eleven are presented here, including places where Johann Sebastian Bach and Paul Gerhardt worked—and it is growing weekly. The route is intended to be navigated on foot, but it is also doable by bicycle and car.

Since the *Lutherweg* is continuously expanding, information is best available online, where it is continuously updated. See the routes and an interactive map at: *www.lutherweg.de*

Wörlitz

The originally Romanesque **Church of St. Peter** (St. Petri-Kirche) was consecrated in 1201. Under Prince Franz of Anhalt-Dessau, it became neo-Gothic. The platform on the 216-foot steeple offers a delightful view. Luther preached here to the Ascanian princes in 1532. The steeple houses a Bible museum.Kirchgasse 34, D-06786 Wörlitz
Phone: +49 (0) 34905–20 09 3
www.gartenreichkirchen.de, www.bibelturm.de

Rosslau

The **Church of St. Mary** (St.-Marien-Kirche), dates back to a church located here in Luther's day, and the Reformer spent many a night in the vicinity. The existing church was built in 1854, and houses a 1,000-year-old baptismal bell.
Grosse Marktstrasse 9, D-06862 Rosslau
Phone: +49 (0) 34901–94 93 30
www.kirche-rosslau.de

Dessau

The **Wörlitz Garden Realm**, a UNESCO World Heritage Site, was created under Franz of Anhalt-Dessau, (1740-1817) and is an excellent example of an Enlightenment Age garden.
Schloss Grosskühnau
Ebenhanstrasse 8
D-06846 Dessau-Rosslau
Phone:
+49 (0) 340–646 150
www.gartenreich.com

Also in **Dessau**:

The **Georgium Palace** houses the Art Museum of Anhalt (Gemäldegalerie), with works of Albrecht Dürer and Lucas Cranach. Above is Cranach's *Marriage of St Catherine*.
Puschkinallee 100, D-06846 Dessau
Phone: +49 (0) 3 40–66 12 60 00; *www.georgium.de*

Church of St. John (St.-Johannis-Kirche). Displayed inside are three paintings from Lucas Cranach the Elder.
Johannisstrasse 11, D-06844 Dessau
Phone: +49 (0) 3 40–21 49 75, *www.johanniskirche-dessau.de*

The **Johannbau Palace**, a former royal residence with an exhibition about the culture and history of Anhalt.
Schlossplatz 3a, D-06844 Dessau
Phone: +49 (0) 3 40–2 20 96 12, *www.stadtgeschichte.dessau.de*

Zerbst

The **Holy Trinity Church** (St.-Trinitatis-Kirche), a Baroque-era building, and the adjacent Gothic-era Church of St. Nicholas (St. Nicolai-Kirche). Formerly the largest church in Anhalt, St. Nicholas was heavily damaged in World War II.
Rennstrasse 7, D-39261 Zerbst
Phone: +49 (0) 3923–48 72 36; *www.sanktnicolai-zerbst.de*

Köthen

The **Church of St. James** (St.-Jakobs-Kirche) and the Bach Memorial (Bach-Gedenkstätte) are also along the trail. Bach was musical director (*Kapellmeister*), in Köthen from 1717 to 1723. This Late Gothic church dates back to 1518. It became Lutheran because of the reigning Prince Wolfgang of Anhalt, who was Lutheran as well. In the crypt are tombs from various family lines of princes. One of them is the tomb of Prince Leopold (1694–1728), who was often called "Bach's Prince."

Hallesche Strasse 15a, D-06366 Köthen
Phone: +49 (0) 3496–21 41 57, *www.jakobskirche-koethen.de*

The **Bach Memorial** is located in the Köthen Palace (Schloss Köthen). The world-famous composer and musician served here as court music director for Prince Leopold of Anhalt-Köthen. The Ludwigsbau contains an exhibition with information on Bach's work.
Schlossplatz 4, D-06366 Köthen
Phone: +49 (0) 34 96–21 25 46
www.kulturstaetten-koethen.de

Wohlsdorf Church (Wohlsdorfer Kirche), a Romanesque structure, features at its entrance a cross of the Order of the Knights Templar. This church was reformed in 1518, and is presently not in use, though there are plans to revive it again.
Dorfstrasse, D-06408 Wohlsdorf
Phone: +49 (0) 3 47 22–3 10 57

Bernburg

Home of **Schloss Bernburg,** the castle on the Saale of the princes and, later, of the dukes of Anhalt, Bernburg. In the Schlossmuseum), sights include reliefs of Lutheran princes.
Schlossstrasse 24, D-06406 Bernburg (Saale)
Phone: +49 (0) 34 71–62 50 07
www.museumschlossbernburg.de

The **Church of St. Mary** (St.-Marienkirche), a Gothic edifice, was first documented in 1228. Prince Wolfgang introduced the Reformation here in 1526.
Breite Strasse 81, D-06406 Bernburg (Saale)
Phone: +49 (0) 34 71–35 36 13
www.bernburger-marienkirche.de

Wettin

The **City Church of St. Nicholas** (St. Nikolai) dates from the 13th century and was modified to Lutheran standards.
Nikolaikirchplatz, D-06198 Wettin
Phone: +49 (0) 34607–20 43 4, *www.nikolaikirche-wettin.de*
Wettin Castle (Burg Wettin), now a ruin, is the ancestral home of the House of Wettin, the dynasty of Frederick the Wise and John Frederick I that ruled Saxony.
Burgstrasse 5, D-06193 Wettin

Brehna

The **Church of St. James** (St.-Jakobs-Kirche), was once part of a Romanesque cloister complex. Katharina von Bora was a pupil here. Today, the church is a roadside chapel (*Autobahnkirche*), that invites travelers to stay for a while.
Bahnhofstrasse 8, D-06796 Brehna
Phone: +49 (0) 33 49 54–4 82 09
www.autobahnkirche-brehna.de

Kemberg

This small town near Wittenberg was often the destination of Luther's ecclesiastical visitations. In 1521, Luther's friend Provost Bernhardi from Kemberg was the first clergyman to marry, thus establishing the first Lutheran parsonage.
Kreuzstrasse 8, D-06901 Kemberg
Phone: +49 (0) 33 49 21–2 04 07, Lampadius@web.de

Grafenhainichen

Here is the **Paul Gerhardt Chapel** (Paul Gerhardt-Kappelle), in the town where the great writer of Lutheran hymns was born. The Classicism-era chapel houses an exhibition about Paul Gerhardt and a library.
Breitscheidstrasse 7, D-06773 Grafenhainichen
Phone: +49 (0) 33 49 53–3 57 57; *www.graefenhainichen.de*

The Wartburg in Eisenach. This famous German castle, over a thousand years old, is where Luther translated the Bible from Latin into German, for the first time. Today, the Wartburg is a museum.

Chapter Five

Luther's Bible

From the Wartburg to Weimar: Traces in Thuringia

On April 16, 1521, Worms—an impressive city with a population of 7,000 already—was full of visitors. Tension was in the air because people knew that Luther was going to give a reply before young Emperor Charles V at the Imperial Diet. Elector Frederick the Wise of Saxony, Luther's protector, had arranged it, against papal opposition.

It was Luther's third debate with his papal opponents, after Augsburg and Leipzig, and he had an even larger audience in imperial Worms. Luther's journey turned into a triumphal procession. His former university in Erfurt had welcomed him enthusiastically beforehand, and his monastic church was "standing room only" as he preached there.

Twice, Luther tried to explain his views to the Imperial Diet, but each time he was emphatically asked to recant. As a result, he replied with a long Latin speech, which he concluded with the famous words:

"Since Your Imperial Highness and Your Majesties desire a plain answer, I will give you such an answer without any horn or teeth. Unless I am convicted by the testimony of Scripture and clear reasoning, for I trust neither the Pope nor councils alone, since it is well known that they have often erred and contradicted themselves, my conscience is bound to the passages in Holy Scripture I have cited. I am held captive by the Word of God. Hence, I cannot and will not retract anything, because it is neither safe nor salutary to go against conscience."

In German he added, "God help me. Amen."

A Prison in the Wartburg

While Luther's words at Worms are still remembered and revered today, Charles V was most certainly not amused. Subsequently, in the infamous Edict of Worms, he imposed on Luther the status of an outlaw.

This meant immediate danger for Luther, but the Elector was still on hand to protect him. On his way home, once Luther was in the territory of Saxony, he was abducted and brought to Wartburg Castle, near Eisenach, in a fake raid carried out by the Elector's men. Living there under the false name of "Knight George" (Junker Jörg), Luther let his hair and beard grow out and was soon no longer recognizable.

Literally a prisoner, Luther was not allowed to leave the vicinity of the castle. Eating food he was not used to and with the lack of activities, he initially did not enjoy his sojourn at all. On August 15, 1521, he wrote to his friend Georg Spalatin from the Wartburg:

> "Last Monday [August 12], I went hunting for two days to see what this bittersweet pleasure of 'heroes' is like. We caught two rabbits and several poor partridges—truly a worthy occupation for men with nothing to do! I theologized even among the snares and dogs. As enjoyable as this endeavor may seem at first glance, however, there was just as much pity and grief that a comparison mixed into it. For what does this picture signify other than that the devil hunts animals that are similarly innocent? But instead of snares and dogs, the devil uses godless teachers and, more specifically, bishops and theologians."

This extremely depressing comparison to simple and believing souls upset Luther very much. But an even more dreadful comparison followed.

> "Because of my efforts, we kept a little rabbit alive. I wrapped it in the sleeve of my coat and left it alone for a while. Meanwhile, the dogs flushed out the poor rabbit.

Biting it through my coat, they first broke its right hind paw and then extinguished its life by a bite to the throat. The Pope (and Satan too!) rages in the exact same way: once again, he ruins souls that are already saved and does not care in the least about my efforts."

After his attitude had improved somewhat, Luther began translating the New Testament, placing great emphasis on using language that would be as easy as possible to understand. He consulted Spalatin and Melanchthon as editors during his stays in Wittenberg. Striving for precision and clarity, he even had the Elector's treasures brought in for study, in order to better translate the various jewels referred to in Revelation 21:18–21. Melanchthon had the task of converting the value of terms for ancient coins as accurately as possible.

As mentioned previously, the "September Testament" sold out and was out of print within a short period of time. In his preface to the New Testament, Luther wrote:

"So, too, the Gospel of God and the New Testament resonated from the apostles into the whole world as the Good News and as a proclamation of victory by the true David who battled with sin, death, and the devil and overcame them. And in so doing, He redeemed, justified, made alive, and saved all who had been held captive in sin, plagued by death, and overwhelmed by the devil—even though they had not merited their salvation. In that way, He made satisfaction for them and brought them back home to God again. For this reason, they sing, thank, and praise God and are eternally glad, as long as they firmly believe [the Gospel] and remain steadfast in the faith."

Of the four Gospels, Luther had the highest esteem for the Gospel of John. In his preface to the New Testament, Luther wrote, "[The Gospels] are the true and noblest books of the New Testament," (after the 1534 edition of the Bible and the 1539 extra edition of the New Testament, this part is left out). Luther justified his statement:

Traveling in the Middle Ages

Traveling was not pleasant in the era of the Reformation. Travelers were exposed to the elements and could be in grave danger just from bad weather. Roads were dilapidated, even though they were continually improved. Detours and longer waiting periods were common. Traveling depended upon the weather and the political situation, and there were very few bridges.

Trails for pack animals led through mountains, and such passes were numerous. In addition, most of the trails were quite difficult to travel and almost impassable in winter. In many cases, traveling was possible only with the assistance of hired guides. With good road conditions, one could cover as many as sixty kilometers (about thirty-seven miles), in one day. On average, however, it was about twenty to forty kilometers (about twelve to twenty-five miles), especially for an inexperienced traveler.

Inns were located along the routes at an interval of three to five old German miles, corresponding to an average day's journey of twenty to forty kilometers (an old German mile is less than five miles).

"Since John writes only a little about the deeds of Christ but quite a lot about His preaching—as opposed to the other three Gospels, which describe many of His deeds but few of His words—John's Gospel is the unmatched, precious, true chief Gospel and by far is preferable to the other three Gospels."

Not only was Luther's translation a theological milestone, it was also a milestone for linguistic history in general. Luther's language was influenced by the dialects of East Middle German and Low German, which were understood by a widespread readership. Because of this, Luther's Bible translation and other works had many readers.

Luther's linguistic contributions impacted the German

> Sea travel was more comfortable and often faster than travel by land. River voyages were relatively safe, though whirlpools, bridge supports, rocks, and rapids threatened the well-being of the travelers. Nights were spent on land.
>
> As with other German codes of law, the Saxon Code (*Sachsenspiegel*) required travelers to stay on the roads. While traveling, one had to be on guard: holdups and ambushes were common, but simple clothing reduced the risk. Often, groups of travelers banded together for safety reasons. In many regions, it was also an option to hire an official armed escort provided by the ruler—for a suitable fee. In addition, travelers would have to pay customs at quite a few customs stations. Pilgrims were generally exempt from these custom fees, as were merchants, depending on their nationality. Mutual exemption from customs was common for the purpose of opening up markets.
>
> Pilgrims could travel without money. But other travelers had to pay not only for customs and accommodations, but also for coachmen, ship captains, guides, or navigators. Those traveling with horses had to expect high costs, since food, stable rental, transportation (crossing rivers, for example), and care consumed large sums of money.

language in a significant way—and are noticeable even in our day and age. For instance, expressions he coined are still used today, such as a Greek phrase, which he rendered as *Wes des Herz voll ist, des geht der Mund über* ("Out of the abundance of the heart the mouth speaks"). Luther's impact and the circulation of his works by the printing press can best be compared to the impact of the Internet. Luther himself had the following opinion on translation:

"I did not use any specific, particular, distinct German dialect. Rather, I used the common speech, so that both upper Germans and lower Germans could understand me. I use the language of Saxon officials, of all the princes and kings in Germany."

SIGHTS AT THE WARTBURG

The Wartburg Castle was first documented in 1080. It belonged to the noble family of the Ludowingians. The historically renowned palace was added between 1156 and 1162, after which the Wartburg changed hands.

The Wartburg is a classic example of a linear castle. Originally composed of four sections, of which only the front and main castle remain today, the Wartburg was besieged many times, yet never conquered. It was made famous by two of its residents—Martin Luther and St. Elizabeth of Thuringia—and it is one of Germany's national monuments. For the Luther anniversary, the Wartburg features a special exhibit, "*Luther and the Germans.*"

SLEEPING AT LUTHER'S

Möhra, the tiny village where the Luther family is originally from, is located just about five miles south of the Wartburg. Möhra offers accomodation for visitors at the house where the Luther family supposedly resided (or, at least, where people in the Luther era lived). More at:

www.thueringen.info/luther-stammhaus-moehra.html

The Wartburg is also famous for the *Sängerkrieg*, a contest of six minstrel singers that supposedly took place here around 1200. It was about praising the Count and even more so the Countess of Thuringia and involved a lot of drama, made immortal by Richard Wagner's opera *Tannhäuser*.

THE DEVIL AND THE INKPOT

The room in which Luther translated the Bible still exists and is part of the museum today. It is here where, legend has it, he threw the ink pot to the devil who bothered him. The ink stain remained permanently for many centuries. Even though visitors kept taking little pieces of ink-stained clay, the stain reappeared mysteriously the next morning, all through the Late Middle Ages, up to the fall of the GDR. It was rumored that the devil himself would reappear during the night to make that happen. It was only after new management took over in the 1990s that the ink stain disappeared.

ELIZABETH OF THURINGIA

Elizabeth was born in Hungary in 1207, and died in Marburg on November 17, 1231. The daughter of King Andrew II of Hungary and Gertrude of Carinthia-Andechs-Merania, Elizabeth was born in the year when the famous "Wartburg Contest"—a competition among troubadours—took place at Wartburg Castle near Eisenach. According to poems and legends, sorcerer Klingsor of Hungary visited the castle and prophesied that the king would have a daughter, namely Elizabeth.

Ludwig IV, son of the Landgrave of Thuringia, married Elizabeth in 1221, when she was only fourteen. Their happy marriage was blessed with three children, the youngest of whom was Gertrude. In 1225, the first Franciscans came to Eisenach. They idealized poverty, making a huge impression on Elizabeth and prompting her to care for the poor. Although her husband supported her, her family viewed her actions with great suspicion. But detailed legends describe how Elizabeth would not be deterred by the slander and criticism of those close to her.

Various miracles are accredited to St. Elizabeth. For example, she supposedly once let a leprous man rest in her marital bed, but when the sheets were pulled back, not the leprous man but the crucified Christ Himself became visible.

1226 was the year of a great famine. Elizabeth had all available grain distributed to the people and even provided money from the treasury for them. When she was vehemently accosted, it is said that the floor of the great hall was suddenly covered with grain and that all of the storehouses overflowed with grain as well. When Emperor Frederick II came to visit with his entourage, Elizabeth could not find an appropriate gown in her wardrobe to wear. Suddenly, an angel adorned Elizabeth with jewels and such splendor that she looked more majestic than anyone in the room.

While the "miracle of the roses" is not documented, the story goes like this: Elizabeth was traveling into the valley, carrying a carefully covered basket full of bread. Incited by his court to check once again on her wastefulness, Frederick II supposedly came up to her and asked, "What are you carrying?" She uncovered the basket, and he saw nothing but roses.

Recruited for the Fifth Crusade, Elizabeth's husband joined the German Order. However, Ludwig fell ill during the voyage off the coast of Brindisi, Italy. After he was brought ashore at Otranto, he died of a disease. Because the Italian Empress Jolantha died at the same place, legend has it that both Ludwig and the empress had consumed a deadly poison together. In her tremendous grief, Elizabeth cried out, "It is to me as if the world died with him."

After Ludwig's death, she and her three children were thrown out of Wartburg Castle by her brother-in-law, Heinrich Raspe, who claimed she was wasting public money on alms. In 1229, Elizabeth moved to Marburg, where her confessor, Conrad of Marburg, lived, a monk belonging to the extremely strict order of the Premonstratensians. Because of his fanatical severity, he was killed in 1233. Elizabeth, however, lived in extreme poverty because she considered it to be virtuous. She went begging from door to door and was determined to relinquish in a final, legally binding manner all of the wealth to which the law entitled her. However, to save the wealth for himself, Conrad prevented her from legally relinquishing it. Consequently, Elizabeth used the funds to build a hospital in Marburg in 1229, which she named after St. Francis. She left her children, joined the hospital society run by Conrad, and worked in the hospital as a nurse until she died at the age of twenty-four. Eliabeth was buried at the St. Francis Hospital she founded.

Elizabeth was canonized only four years after her death. In a vision of Mechthild of Helfta, God Himself is said to have justified her canonization, explaining, "My messengers need to be quick. Elizabeth was and is a messenger whom I sent to women who sit around in castles, are full of selfish pride, arrogant, completely immoral, and wrapped up in vanity. They do not worry about their salvation one little bit. In fact, these women are so wicked that they deserve to go to hell. On the other hand, many other women have followed the example of Elizabeth, as far as their willpower and strength will let them."

Later, the German Order based in Marburg expanded Elizabeth's hospital and built Germany's first Gothic building between 1235 and 1283, a church dedicated to her.

The Luther House in Eisenach. The half-timbered house actually belonged to the Cotta family. According to an old tradition, Martin Luther lived in this house while attending school in Eisenach from 1498 to 1501.

An Early Home in Eisenach

For Luther, his involuntary Wartburg stay was not the first time he had resided in the city of Eisenach. It was here where young Luther spent happy years at the Latin School, right after his year in Magdeburg. This is also the reason he called the town, "Eisenach, my dear city."

When Luther arrived in Eisenach, he was only fifteen and lived with relatives at first. At the time, young Luther earned his sustenance by singing in front of homes and being rewarded with bread. This was common for pupils of that era.

Later Heinrich Schalbe, mayor from 1495 to 1499, took him in. Schalbe's son was about the same age as Luther and attended the same school, St. George's, named after the neighboring church. Here, Luther participated in the cult of St. Anne, which was extremely popular at that time. Luther's beloved teacher, Johannes Braun, and many of his fellow students took part in it as well. Luther stayed in contact with his teacher even after entering the monastery. During this period, his deep sense of Catholic piety was formed.

In the 150 years before Luther's arrival, once-flourishing Eisenach had experienced a steep decline in population, to some 4,000 people. In 1342, the town nearly burned down, followed by two outbreaks of the plague. In 1406, Margrave Balthazar died, so Eisenach was no longer a capital with the prince's residence. There were still more clergy in Eisenach during that period, however, than would have been customary for an average city. Eisenach had three parish churches: the Church of St. Nicholas, the Church of St. George, and the Church of St. Mary (Marienstift). On top of that, the Dominicans, Franciscans, and Carthusians all had monasteries in town. So religious life was rich and multifaceted.

Eisenach recovered, except for a setback during the Thirty Years' War. Today, Eisenach is mostly known as the town where Johann Sebastian Bach was born, on March 21, 1685, as the son of a local musician. That house is now a museum.

Sights in Eisenach

Luther House (Lutherhaus)

Beginning in 1898, the building was the home of the Luther Keller, a restaurant specializing in traditional German cuisine. Both of Luther's rooms have been open to the public since then. Damaged in World War II, the building was repaired, and the State Church of Thuringia established a Luther memorial there in 1956.

Luther Monument (Lutherdenkmal)

This larger-than-life statue is located on Karlsplatz. Constructed by Adolf Donndorf in 1895, it depicts events from Luther's life. His famous hymn, *"A Mighty Fortress,"* is engraved here.

Church of St. George (Georgenkirche)

The Church of St. George was built in the 12th century and is where St. Elizabeth got married. Luther preached here shortly after the beginning of the Reformation, in May,

1521, so it became one of the oldest Lutheran churches in the world. St. George's was destroyed in the Peasants' War, but rebuilt and dedicated again in 1558. Johann Sebastian Bach, who was born in Eisenach, was also baptized in this church, in 1685. The baptismal font from his era is still present. A new steeple was built around 1900.

THE CULT OF ST. ANNE

According to the apocryphal Gospels (the false Gospels written between the 2nd and 6th centuries AD). Anne and Joachim were the parents of Mary and, as such, the grandparents of Jesus. Anne gave birth to Mary after twenty years of barren marriage. From the 6th century on, Anne was venerated as the mother of Mary.

In Europe, the cult of Anne peaked in the Late Middle Ages, when in 1481, Pope Sixtus IV included a day of commemoration for Anne in the calendar of the Catholic Church. In 1584, Pope Gregory XIII designated July 26 as her festival day. Supposedly from 1500 on, relics. of St. Anne were kept in Duren, Vienna, and elsewhere.

St. Anne is the patron saint of thunderstorms. Around St. Anne's Day in late July, the "dog days of summer" begin, lasting until early August. This time of year is determined by the rise of Sirius, the "Dog Star," in the constellation of Canis Major (Great Dog). Heat waves, which trigger thunderstorms, are common during this time of year.

Bach House (Bachhaus)

Johann Sebastian Bach is Eisenach's most famous son. The Bachhaus, however, the family's half-timbered home from 1646–48, was not where he was born; parts of his family resided here, but the actual house is long gone. The Bachhaus has been a museum since 1907, with a new extension built in 2007. It contains furniture and a stove from Bach's day, along with a collection of organs and pianos. The Museum organizes concerts on the hour.

Addresses and Travel Information

Tourist Information
Am Markt 24 im Stadtschloss, D-99817 Eisenach
Phone: +49 (0) 3691–79 23 0
www.eisenach.info, info@eisenach.info

Luther House (Lutherhaus)
Lutherplatz 8, D-99817 Eisenach
Phone: +49 (0) 3691–29 83 0, +49 (0) 176–21 39 11 14
www.lutherhaus-eisenach.de, info@lutherhaus-eisenach.de

Luther Monument (Lutherdenkmal)
Karlsplatz, D-99817 Eisenach
Phone: +49 (0) 3691–79 23 0
www.eisenach.info, info@eisenach.info

Church of St. George (Georgenkirche)
Am Markt, D-99817 Eisenach
Phone: +49 (0) 3691–79 23 0
eisenach-1@kirchenkreis-eisenach.de

Bach House (Bachhaus)
Frauenplan 21, D-99817 Eisenach
Phone: +49 (0) 3691–79 34 0
www.bachhaus.de, info@bachhaus.de

Hotels in Eisenach

City Hotel Eisenach ***
Bahnhofstrasse 25, D-99817 Eisenach
Phone: +49 (0) 36 91–20 98 0
info@cityhotel-eisenach.de
www.cityhotel-eisenach.de

Lutherhotel Eisenacher Hof ****
Katharinenstrasse 13, D-99817 Eisenach
Phone: +49 (0) 3691–29 39 0
www.hotel-eisenach.com, info@eisenacherhof.de

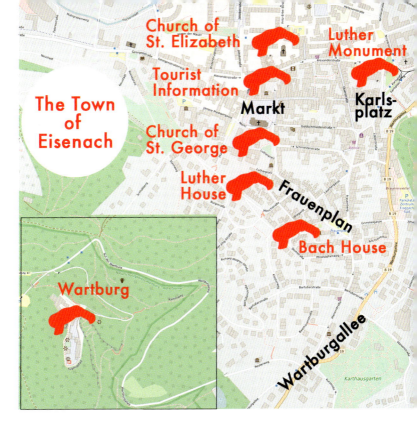

The Wartburg is on a mountain just outside of Eisenach, about a 30 minutes walk. Alternatively, cabs and bus No. 10 or 13 leave from the train station. From the base of the castle, it's a 500-foot walk uphill, but there is a shuttle for the impaired.

Hotels in Eisenach

Haus Hainstein ***
Am Hainstein 16, D-99817 Eisenach
Phone: +49 (0) 3691–2420, *www.haushainstein.de*

Romantik Hotel auf der Wartburg *****
Auf der Wartburg 2, D-99817 Eisenach
Phone: +49 (0) 3691–797 0, info@wartburg.de

ibis Hotel Eisenach ***
Am Grundbach 1, D-99819 Eisenach
Phone: +49 (0) 36920–82100, *www.hotel-eisenach.com*

Sculpted by Berlin artist Fritz Schaper on the occasion of Luther's 400th birthday in 1883, the monument is located on the south side of the Merchants' Church, where Luther preached in October 1521. It is eighteen feet high and depicts the Reformer carrying a Bible.

As A Monk In Erfurt

The first officially recorded date in Luther's life is his student attendance at the University of Erfurt in 1501, which reads, "*Martinus Ludher ex Mansfeld.*" This is how we know that Luther began his studies that year. Before swearing his oath to the dean and the university, Luther had to pay his tuition of one third of a guilder because the registrar's office considered him to be well off (i*n habendo*).

After only three semesters, Luther earned the first degree of medieval university instructors, the *baccalaureat artibus,* which was a kind of assistantship in the so-called seven liberal arts. These arts included mathematics, music, astronomy, and rhetoric, skills that had to be acquired before one could continue his education.

Luther was full of praise for Erfurt: "Erfurt has an excellent location in the fat of the land. That is where a city should be located—even if it were to burn down."

Erfurt, founded in 742 AD, was an economic center on the major trade routes within the lowlands of Thuringia. With a population of about 20,000 in Luther's day, it was one of the largest cities in Germany. Its university was founded in 1392, and demonstrated confidence and economic strength. It was one of the first universities in Germany, was self regulated, and had an increasingly good reputation.

Students tended to live in dormitories called *Bursen*. This was true for Luther as well, who lived in a dormitory called the "gateway to Heaven" (*Himmelspforte*) during his first two years of college, one of the most prestigious dorms in town. The house rules were about as strict as those in a monastery. The residents, so called *Bursalen*, wore clothing according to their academic level. In the *Bursen*, students wore a vest, long trousers and a belt. In public, a coat or robe was worn over the outfit, in addition to a head covering. Students were required to study very hard and to speak Latin, even outside of class. "Carousing and relationships with the other sex" were prohibited, though the *Bursen* were allowed to serve alcohol during the hours of operation customary for taverns.

Life was spartan in the *Bursen*. The students slept in sleeping halls. Seven students shared a workroom. They had to wake up at 4 a.m. and went to bed at 8 p.m. Only two meals a day were served. Breakfast was at 10 a.m. and the second meal was after lectures, at 5 p.m. Classes began at 8 a.m. Students attended the church services of the university and of their faculty, and spiritual life continued in the *Bursen*.

In 1505, Luther became a *magister*, which means he got a master's degree in liberal arts. This academic rank was similar to that of an associate professor today. In his master's examination at the end of the year, Luther ranked second in a class of seventeen. In accordance with his father's wishes, Luther began his law studies on May 19, beginning first with civil law. However, on July 17—less than two months later—he joined the Augustinian order. Luther had experienced a crisis after some of his colleagues and professors suddenly died of the plague and other diseases. Yet there was also another incident, one that would change his life forever.

How to get to Thuringia

With a population of about 210,000, Erfurt is the largest city in Thuringia and its capital. In World War II, it was heavily damaged. The city was occupied by General Patton's troops, who handed it to the Soviets. Since the Wall came down, Erfurt has been splendidly rebuilt--not only the churches, but landmarks such as the historical Krämerbrücke (Merchants' Bridge), synagogue, and fish market as well.

Erfurt is a hub of transportation, especially for high-speed trains. Eisenach, Gotha, Weimar, and Jena are connected by the ICE from Frankfurt to Leipzig; Eisenach is connected to the regional Werrabahn and the Thüringer Bahn to Halle. Starting in December 2017, the ICE from Berlin to Munich will run through Erfurt. Autobahn A 4 from Frankfurt to Dresden also connects Erfurt to those cities

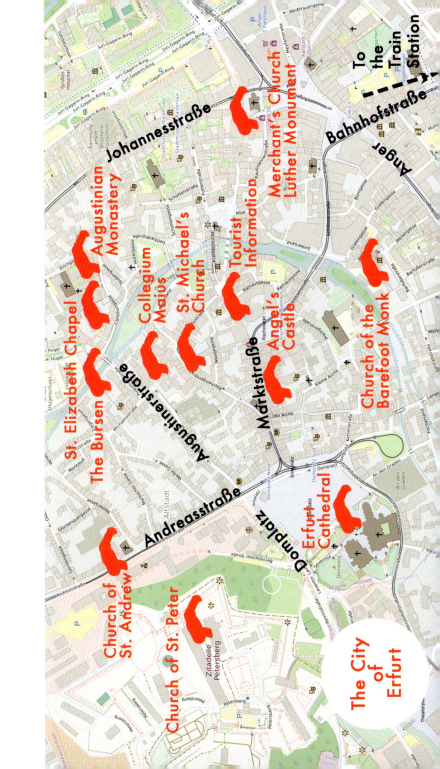

Sights in Erfurt

Augustinian Monastery and St. Elizabeth Chapel (Augustinerkloster und St. Elisabeth Kapelle)

The first Parish Church of Saints Philipp and James was constructed in 1131, at the site where the monastery now stands. In 1266, the Augustinians received permission to establish a presence. Construction of today's building began in 1277, funded by alms and indulgences. By 1518, the monastery included an impressive library, the Chapel of St. Catherine, the chapter house, a steeple, a cloister with a nave and a priory, and wood storehouses.

Luther was a member of the monastery from 1505 to 1511, and he read his first Mass here on May 2, 1507. Because the

order had its own college, the Augustinians became the first theology professors when Erfurt University was founded. Luther attended Erfurt University from 1501 to 155.

The monastery was secularized during the Reformation. In 1561, the city built a secondary school in the west wing. In World War II, part of the Augustian, including the library, were destroyed by British bombers. After the Iron Curtain fell in 1989, the monastery was renovated. Since then, nuns of the Community Casteller Ring have breathed new life into the monastery. Visitors can now be housed in one of fifty rooms renovated with the look and feel of medieval monasteries.

Next to the monastery is the St. Elizabeth Chapel within the tower of St. Nicholas, dating back to 1212. The ground floor is adorned with secco murals, which are among the very few 14th-century murals that still exist in Germany.

The Bursen (Georgenburse)

Not much is left of the *Bursen*, where Luther lived as a student, except this historic marker, and a few bare walls. A small exhibit is currently being prepared for the Luther year..

Church of St. Andrew (Andreaskirche)

This church from 1210 is the gate to the Andreas District. The interior is adorned with a large wooden panel with a color frame, depicting a relief of Luther. This panel was the template for Luther's bronze gravestone in Wittenberg.

Church of St. Peter (Peterskirche)

The Church of St. Peter was originally built as a fortress on Petersberg Hill between 1665 and 1726. It was later remodeled for the military, and is now a museum for the arts.

Erfurt Cathedral

Luther was ordained as a priest in this cathedral, named for St. Mary. It is believed that a sanctuary was erected at this site in 752. The cathedral was first documented in 1117. Some sections of the original church—built in the Romanesque style—still exist today. However, since the church was soon deemed too small for the  growing number of clerics, it was continually expanded, but in the Gothic style. The cathedral is famous for its many stained-glass windows and ancient murals. The cathedral was damaged in various wars, but never completely destroyed. In 1994, it was designated as the cathedral of the newly reestablished Catholic Diocese.

Angel's Castle (Engelsburg)

The Engelsburg is a row of buildings, some up to 900 years old, where Luther stayed, once when he was sick. Today, it is a cultural center for graduate students.

Old University (Alte Universität) and Collegius Maius

The university is situated in the Latin Quarter within historic structures reminiscent of the old university. One is the Collegium Maius—the main bulding—which was destroyed in World War II, but has been undergoing reconstruction since 1998. The university was built between 1512 and 1515, and its motto is still legible, chiseled in stone above the portal. "*Magistra vitae regina rerumpossidet sapientia*," which means. "Wisdom—the teacher of life and queen of the world—rules here."

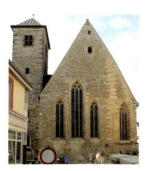

St Michael's Church (Michaeliskirche)

This 13th-century parish church is one of the most beautiful Gothic churches, with the oldest bell, dating from 1380. Luther preached here many times. The church, heavily damaged in World War II, has been restored.

Church of the Barefoot Monks (Barfüsserkirche)

Built in 1231, this church originally belonged to a Franciscan monastery. Luther preached here in 1529. The church was destroyed by Allied bombing in 1944, although the stained-glass windows from 1230–1240 had been secured beforehand. The ruins were preserved. In 2012, they were adorned with a relief, "Dance of Death," created by artist Hans Walther in 1947.

ADDRESSES AND TRAVEL INFORMATION

Tourist Information
Benediktsplatz 1, D-99084 Erfurt
Phone: +49 (0) 361–66 40 0, *www.erfurt-tourismus.de*

Luther Monument and Kaufmannskirche
Anger 80, D-99084 Erfurt
Phone: +49 (0) 361–26 26 96 2
www.evkaufmannsgemeinde.de

Augustinian Monastery and St. Elisabeth Chapel
Augustinerstrasse 10, D-99084 Erfurt
Phone: +49 (0) 361–57 66 00
www.augustinerkloster.de, info@augustinerkloster.de

The Bursen (Georgenbörse)
Augustinerstrasse 27, D-99084 Erfurt
Phone: +49 (0) 361–57 66 09 4
www.augustinerkloster.de/georgenburse

Church of St. Andrew (Andreaskirche)
Andreasstrasse 14, D-99084 Erfurt
Phone: +49 (0) 361–21 15 23 9
www.andreasgemeinde-erfurt.de

Church of St. Peter (Peterskirche)
Petersberg 14, D-99084 Erfurt
Phone: +49 (0) 361–65 51 61 1
www.thueringerschloesser.de

Erfurt Cathedral
Domstufen 1, D-99084 Erfurt
Phone: +49 (0) 361–57 69 60
www.dom-erfurt.de, pfarramt@domberg-erfurt.de

Angel's Castle (Engelsburg)
Allerheiligenstrasse 20/21, D-99084 Erfurt
Phone: +49 (0) 361–24 47 70; *www.eburg.de*

Old University (Alte Universität) and Collegius Maius
Michaelisstrasse, D–99084 Erfurt
Phone: +49 (0) 361–66 40 0
www.erfurt-tourismus.de, info@erfurt-tourismus.de

St Michael's Church (Michaeliskirche)
Michaelisstrasse 11, D–99084 Erfurt
Phone: +49 (0) 361–64 22 09 0

Church of the Barefooted Monks (Barfüsserkirche)
Barfüsserstrasse 20, D-99084 Erfurt
Phone: +49 (0) 361–65 51 65 1, *www.barfuesserkirche.d*e

Hotels in Erfurt

Arcadia Grand Hotel Am Dom Erfurt *****
Theaterplatz 2, D-99084 Erfurt
Phone: +49 (0) 361–64450, info.erfurt@ahmm.de

Hotel Zumnorde **** superior
Anger 50 – 51, D-99084 Erfurt
Phone: +49 (0) 361–56800, info@hotel-zumnorde.de

Radisson Blu Erfurt ****
Juri Gagarin Ring 127, D-99084 Erfurt
Phone: +49 (0) 361–55100, info@radission-erfurt.com

Mercure Hotel Erfurt-Altstadt ****
Meienbergstr. 26–27, D-99084 Erfurt
Phone: +49 (0) 361–59490, h5375@accor.com

Hotel Krämerbrücke Erfurt ****
Gotthardstr. 27, D-99084 Erfurt
Phone: +49 (0) 361–67400,
info@hotel-kraemerbrücke.de

Best Western Plus Hotel Excelsior ****
Bahnhofstr. 35, D-99084 Erfurt
Phone: +49 (0) 361–56700
info@excelsior.bestwestern.de

In 1917, a stone made of Swedish granite and donated by a resident was erected where sources suggest that Luther pleaded with St. Anne in Stotternheim. It became a place for pilgrims. It is one train stop—ten minutes—north of Erfurt.

Lightning in Stotternheim

In June 1505, Luther traveled to Mansfeld to visit his parents. Returning to Erfurt on July 2, he was caught in a violent thunderstorm near the village of Stotternheim, located just below the Stollberg range of hills and some six kilometers (four miles) from Erfurt. A bolt of lightning struck the ground near him, probably knocking him down and injuring his leg. Scared to death, he swore, "Help me, St. Anne. I will become a monk." He later said that he was so afraid of being killed that he was forced to make the oath. He "must have thought there was no way to avoid taking this oath," because—as he always emphasized later—he did not actually want to become a monk. On July 16, Luther celebrated with his friends one last time and bade them farewell. Luther later wrote the following about his Erfurt years:

> "To aspire to a bachelor's degree, yes, even a master's degree, and then to lay down the brown beret, leaving it for others to pursue, and then to become a monk was not the least bit disgraceful. Yet my father became very upset about it. Years later, however, when I had locked horns with the Pope, my father and I made up."

Apparently for more than a decade, Luther was able to reconcile what he read in his mandatory Bible studies in the monastery with the effusive devotion of the Virgin Mary customary in that environment. He strove in all earnest to live as a monk, even testing his physical limitations. Although he accepted the various humiliating tasks assigned to him, he could not hold to all of the rules, despite his diligence. His conscience constantly troubled him, because he could not perfectly complete all the canonical hours and his mandatory duties. At the same time, those activities—along with complete weekly confessions—were meant as works of penance to pay for sins. Luther's superiors at the monastery could not help but notice how intensely Luther studied

Scripture and how diligent and intelligent he was. So after only two years, on February 27, 1507, he was ordained as a priest. This new status reconciled Luther with his father, who traveled to Erfurt for the ordination, in a carriage pulled by a magnificent team of horses.

At that time, the monastery at Erfurt had extremely strict ordinances. They were taken very seriously—as was the order itself—and obeyed by Luther and his fellow monks. Vicar General Johann von Staupitz had the difficult task of maintaining this strict monastic life. He charged Luther and another monk to travel to Rome in order to address the order's regulations. Thus in November 1510, Luther began the longest journey of his life. Traveling southward through Germany, he and his traveling companion stopped at Nuremberg, Ulm, and probably Memmingen. "The journey probably continued along the Rhine valley via Chur and the Septimer Pass to Chiavenna. From there they presumably continued along Lake Como, down to Milan."

On the way, the two men had to cross difficult Alpine passes. In those days, the landscape of Rome had not yet been greatly influenced by the Renaissance. In fact, only a few churches and buildings had been built in that style. Work on St. Peter's Basilica had just begun.

But Luther was more interested in his salvation than in Roman architecture. As had already happened twice in Erfurt, he once again wanted to give a general confession in Rome. But to his disgust, Luther's Roman confessors were not interested in hearing him out. Luther was also greatly disappointed that Masses were being celebrated in a purely mechanical fashion. In fact, within the space of only one hour, he witnessed seven Masses celebrated in the Basilica of St. Sebastian, yet none of them met his expectations.

But those were not the only abuses that he saw—not by a long shot. By exploiting rich monasteries for prebends owed to them, cardinals were awash in luxury, Luther observed. Furthermore, the generally immoral behavior—especially among the clergy—repulsed him.

> ## Ecclesiastical Fight Over Erfurt
>
> Erfurt was the hub of many ecclesiastical institutions, boasting four diocesan churches, twenty-one parish churches, and eleven monastery churches. Towering over these—geographically and in importance—was the residence of a bishop consecrated by Mainz, the diocese cathedral, (Domstift)
>
> Politically, however, the city was not in an enviable position. Both the archbishop of Mainz and the Elector of Saxony were fighting over move influence, trying to hinder Erfurt's independence. Furthermore, in one of the struggles with the archbishop of Mainz, Erfurt unfortunately sided with the opposing, losing party and thus had to declare bankruptcy in 1509. Also in that crazy year, the citizens rebelled against the substantial tax imposed by the four-headed government of the city. In fact, one of its four rulers, Heinrich Keller, was executed the following year. In the next battle, the peasants sided with Mainz, while the upper class took the side of Saxony, as Luther did, when he later returned to Erfurt.

Nevertheless, to a certain extent Rome had captured Luther's heart, and he eagerly did the classic tour, including pilgrimages to each of Rome's seven main churches in a single day, beginning outside the Roman gates at the Church of St. Paul, where the remains of the apostle Paul are entombed. Next came the Church of St. Sebastian along the Via Appia, then the Basilica of St. John Lateran, the Church of the Holy Cross, the Church of St. Lawrence, St. Maria Maggiore, and, finally, St. Peter's Basilica, where a Mass was celebrated. Because they knew they would be attending Mass that evening, every pilgrim on the tour had to fast all day long. Luther also went on pilgrimages to other churches and catacombs, took in all of the history, and read a Mass wherever possible.

Without any concern for his trousers—he considered the Italian styles to be more elegant—Luther crawled up the steps to the Palace of Pilate in the Lateran Palace, praying the

Lord's Prayer on every step. He did all of this to free his grandfather from purgatory. But as soon as he had reached the top step, Luther already began to doubt whether all his effort had been worthwhile. His attempt to resolve the conflict of the order was equally unsuccessful. Thus, in winter 1511, Luther returned to Erfurt without having accomplished anything.

THE TOWER EXPERIENCE

Years later, however, Luther would gain insight in his study in the tower of Wittenberg's Augustinian Monastery, in an event known as the "Tower Experience." Luther's study of the Bible triggered it, and it is regarded as the start of the Reformation. What this means for believers is that God's Word reveals that they are sinners but that they are declared righteous by the Gospel without meeting any requirement. In that way, the just God is also the merciful God in Christ. Here is the insight in Luther's own words:

"To be sure, I was unusually zealous in trying to understand Paul in his Epistle to the Romans. But there was one little phrase in chapter 1, with which I struggled. It was the phrase, 'in it the righteousness of God is revealed.' I hated the phrase 'the righteousness of God' because I had been taught…to understand 'righteousness'…in the sense that God is just and therefore punishes sinners and the unjust. Even though I was living as a blameless monk."

"I felt that before God I was still a sinner with an uneasy conscience. I could not rely on being justified by making my own amends. I was not able to love this 'just' God. In fact, I hated Him because He punishes sinners. When I did not blaspheme out loud, I certainly expressed my outrage at God with vicious murmuring, 'As though it were not quite enough to oppress and afflict us miserable sinners, who are already eternally lost because of original sin, with but one law of the Ten Commandments! On top of this, with the Gospel He has now added fresh pain to our old pain! Even with the Gospel, God is threatening us with His righteous anger!' This caused me to rage, driven by a wild and confused conscience. I ruthlessly kept on beating my head against that particular passage of Paul's. I was hungry and thirsty to find out what St. Paul was trying to say."

"Finally, God showed me mercy. After wracking my brains for days, I suddenly noticed the correlation of the words in the verse: 'For in it the righteousness of God is revealed from faith to faith, as it is written, The righteous shall live by faith.' At that point I began to understand the righteousness of God, namely, that the person who is justified because of a gift of God lives by it and, in fact, by faith. At that point, I felt as if I were completely born again. I felt like I had stepped through an open gate into paradise."

"Suddenly, all of Scripture opened itself up to me seamlessly in a brand-new light. I ran through Scripture by memory and discovered the same concept in other passages: God's work consists in what He works in us. God's power consists in His making us powerful. God's wisdom consists in His making us wise. The same is true for the strength of God, the salvation of God, and the honor of God. Now, as much as I used to hate the righteousness of God, I now lifted up this sweetest of words in my love. In this way, this passage of Paul became the gate to paradise for me."

The Church of St. Margareth (Margarethenkirche). Johann Langenhan preached the gospel in this church in 1522. Larger-than-life statues of Luther and Melanchthon chiseled from sand stone greet visitors at the church entrance (picture right).

Gotha's Gardens

Thuringia is the heartland of Protestantism, and Luther visited many of its towns and cities. They are adorned not only with churches, but also with other places of cultural significance. Gotha has not only a castle dating back more than half a millenium—with a statue of Ernest the Pious in front of it, from the Ernestine branch of the Wettin dukes—but royal gardens, parks, and fountains as well.

Martin Luther visited Gotha many times, partly on official business to see the Augustinian Monastery. Along with Bad Langensalza and Erfurt, Gotha was one of three monasteries established by Augustinian monks. A chapter of the German Augustinian congregations met in Gotha in spring 1515, and installed Martin Luther as district vicar over ten (later eleven) Augustinian convents in Saxony and Thuringia. He apparently approached his duties with a firm hand.

Luther also stopped over in Gotha to confer with his friend Friedrich Myconius, known as the "Gothan Reformer." Myconius was a dedicated Lutheran who was even imprisoned for a short time in 1522. But the boisterous rebel managed to flee to Saxony. He was sent to Gotha as a pastor to bring the Reformation to the people. Gotha became Lutheran early. Not all of Luther's visits were fortunate, however. Once, he fell so gravely ill that he drafted his will.

Gotha is also the hometown of the Bach family. Johannes Bach, great grandfather of Johann Sebastian, was Gotha's city piper. He lived at Market Square. The house is now gone.

Sights in Gotha

Augustinian Monastery and Church (Augustinerkloster)

Despite other uses, the recently restored and modernized monastery is a place of tranquility. The Augustinian Church, where Luther preached many times, was built in 1366. Myconius House, next to the monastery complex (photo left), is Gotha's oldest surviving residential home. Here, Friedrich Myconius lived from 1524 to his death in 1546.

Luther House (Lutherhaus)

The "Lutherhaus" on the market square. On the way home from the diet of princes in nearby Schmalkalden, Luther stopped in Gotha on February 27, 1537. Severe kidney pain kept him bedridden in the Zur Löwenburg Hotel until March 4.

Thinking he was dying, he dictated his will to Reformer Johannes Bugenhagen and discussed his pending burial with Myconius. Today, a café with an upscale pastry shop here.

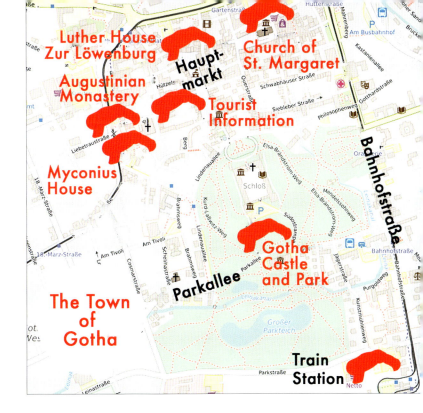

Addresses and Travel Information

Tourist Information
Hauptmarkt 33, D-99867 Gotha
Phone: +49 (0) 3621–74 12 95
www.kultourstadt.de/tourismus.html

The Church of St. Margaret (Margarethenkirche).
Südstrasse 4a, D-99867 Gotha
Phone: +49 (0) 3621–74 12 95, *www.kirchengemeinde-gotha.de*

Augustinian Monastery and Church
Myconius House (Myconiushaus)
Jüdenstrasse 27, D-99867 Gotha
Phone: +49 (0) 3621–30 29 10
www.augustinerkloster-gotha.de

Luther House "Zur Löwenburg" (Lion's Castle)
Hauptmarkt 41, D-99867 Gotha

Martin Luther stayed in this impressive half-timbered building during his sojourn in the city. Because he was sick, Luther met people and also preached there. Luther House, on Market Square, is also where a Martin Luther Trail begins.

Smalcald Articles

Medieval Schmalkalden was a wealthy city, due to its large deposits of iron. During the Reformation, it was at the center stage of European politics. On February 27, 1531, shortly after the death of Swedish Reformer Ulrich Zwingli, nine Protestant princes formed the Schmalkaldic League, led by Landgrave Philipp I of Hessen and Elector John Frederick of Saxony, the Magnanimous. The Elector, who was educated by Georg Spalatin, had a close relationship with Martin Luther and endorsed the Reformation early on. The Schmalkaldic League was a military alliance of Protestant estates against Habsburg Emperor Charles V. Philipp of Hessen, one of the first Protestant princes, was convinced that only an alliance of all Protestants could offer protection.

The Hessian Landgrave Philipp invited members of the Schmalkaldic League to the Diet of Princes in Schmalkalden in February 1537. Sixteen princes, six counts, imperial and papal envoys, royal envoys from the French and Danish kings, and representatives from 28 imperial and Hanseatic cities attended, along with 42 Protestant theologians, including Martin Luther and Philipp Melanchthon. Luther, already one of the most prominent theologians at the time, arrived in the company of the Elector, John Frederick of Saxony. On his order, Luther presented tenets later incorporated as the "Smalcald Articles" into the Book of Concord of the Evangelical Church in 1580. They were "articles by which I must and will stand until I die, God willing, and know of nothing in them to change or concede," Luther wrote in a letter. He had to leave the city earlier than originally planned, because he was "not well for over three days." He wrote to his wife, Katharina, "In short, I was dead."

The League did not achieve long-term success. Soon at serious odds among themselves, the princes lost the Schmalkaldic War of 1546–1547 at Mühlberg. Landgrave Philipp I and Elector John Frederick surrendered in Wittenberg.

Sights in Schmalkalden

Part of Thuringia today, Schmalkalden's historic district is listed on the national register. It was restored after German reunification and is comprised largely of half-timbered buildings from the 14th to 18th centuries. The three-story buildings were built in the Frankish frame construction style.

Market Square with Town Hall and Hessenhof

The town hall on the market square looks like it is comprised of three buildings. The ground floor was once a large hall with open arcades, where markets were held. Between 1530 and 1543, the Protestant theologians of the Schmalkaldic League met six times above the Ratskeller, in what is now known as the Hessenhof, to negotiate tenets of faith—which made the town hall the League's most important meeting center. The city crests of League members in the front hall and the bust of Luther created by Wieland Förster in 1996 allude to the 16th-century events. Rose Apothecary is also here, first used by the *Reitende Post* (mail service on horseback), and as an apothecary since 1664. During the Schmalkaldic League's meeting in 1537, the Nuremberg envoys stayed there.

St. George's Municipal Church

Built from 1437 to 1509, the church is one of the nicest Late Gothic hall churches in Thuringia. In February–March 1537, the most notable Protestant theologians of the time preached in the church, including Martin Luther, who appeared there twice, in February 1537. He stayed in the "Luther Room," the former parament chamber above the sacristy. There is a small church exhibition in the room today. The ornate church windows are particularly beautiful. The best time to visit is late in the afternoon.

Wilhelmsburg Castle

The structure, built by Landgrave William IV from 1585–1589, is a jewel among the Renaissance castles in Germany. The small, newly restored castle perches above the city. A permanent exhibition in the castle museum is also devoted to the Reformation, Martin Luther, and the history of the Schmalkaldic League.

LUTHER'S HEALTH PROBLEMS

Luther commented on his health problems in various letters. On February 27, 1537, he wrote Katie from Tambach:

"I set out from Schmalkalden yesterday and traveled here in my gracious lord's [the Elector's] personal carriage. The reason for this is that the whole time I have been here, I have been unwell for over three days. From last Sunday [February 18] until this evening, not a drop of water passed from me. I could not rest or sleep. I was unable to hold down any food or drink. In short, I was dead and had already commended you, along with the children, to God and my gracious [Elector] and thought I would never see you again in this mortal life. I felt great pity for you, but I had already resigned myself to the grave. But there was so much fervent prayer to God on my behalf and the tears of many people were so effective that God opened my bladder this evening and in two hours at least three to four liters passed from me. I feel like I have been born again."

The history of the Reformer's illnesses is long, and numerous books have been written on it. In particular, reports from the last years of his life frequently mention his state of health. Several illnesses afflicted him, yet he would not reduce his workload. Luther responded to the strict dietary restrictions of doctors with skepticism, since he wanted to enjoy the good gifts of God with thanksgiving. Preventative measures were not what he had in mind. Although it is not confirmed that Luther ever made this statement, there are many variations of what Bertolt Brecht quoted Luther as saying, "I will eat what I like and die when God wills it."

He considered illness to be the work of the devil, and regarded faith and prayer as the best antidotes. He was against renouncing doctors and medicine, however, because it would be "too sinful to tempt God." Nevertheless, Luther did occasionally express that they would need a "new church cemetery" because of all of the doctors' risky treatments. The Reformer's frequent attacks of gout were possibly related to his diet.

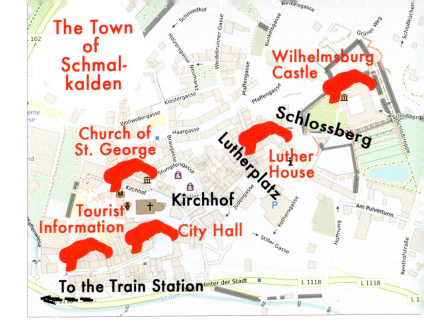

ADDRESSES AND TRAVEL INFORMATION

Tourist Information
Auer Gasse 6–8, D-98574 Schmalkalden
Phone: +49 (0) 3683–60 97 58 0,
www.schmalkalden.com, info@schmalkalden.de

Market Square with City Hall and Hessenhof
Altmarkt 1, D-98574 Schmalkalden
Phone: +49 (0) 3683–60 97 58 0

Lutherhaus Schmalkalden
Lutherplatz 7, D-98574 Schmalkalden
Phone: +49 (0) 36 83–40 31 82

St. George's Municipal Church
Kirchhof 3, D-98574 Schmalkalden
Phone: +49 (0) 3683–40 24 71
www.kirchengemeinde-schmalkalden.de

Wilhelmsburg Castle
Schlossberg 9, D-98574 Schmalkalden
Phone: +49 (0) 3683–40 31 86
www.museumwilhelmsburg.de, info@museumwilhelmsburg.de

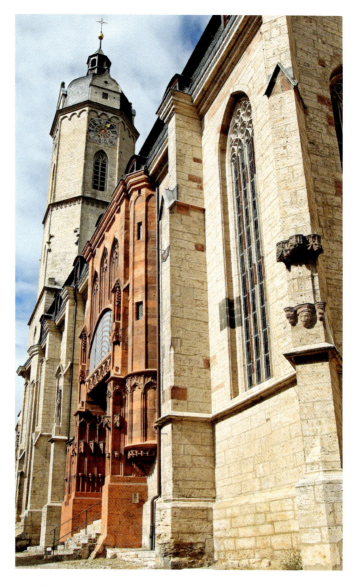

St. Michael's in Jena, the site of the showdown between Luther and Karlstadt, with Luther on the richly decorated pulpit built around 1500. Across from it is the Reformer's original grave plate, by Erfurt sculptor Johann Ziegler.

Showdown in Jena

Between 1522 and 1537, Martin Luther visited Jena at least eleven times, but two of his sojourns were risky as well as unavoidable. They involved his fomer ally Andreas Bodenstein von Karlstadt, who had accompanied Luther to the Leipzig Disputation. While Luther was living at the Wartburg, disguised as "Junker Jörg," Karlstadt took over in bringing the Reformation to Wittenberg. But soon he was accused of being responsible for the "*Bildersturm*," the destruction of pictures, even though he spoke out against violence.

Luther traveled from the Wartburg to Wittenberg on March 3, 1522, to take a stand against Karlstadt, and took lodging in Jena for the first time. He stayed at the "Schwarzer Bär" (Black Bear) Hotel and restaurant, which is still in operation, where he talked to students. In August 1524, Luther headed to Jena for a final showdown with his former friend. In Jena's packed municipal church, with Karstadt hiding in the crowd, Luther gave a ninety-minute sermon. Karlstadt was exiled in 1524, and died in Switzerland in 1541.

In 1548, after the debacle of the Schmalcaldic War, Jena University was founded, as a—somewhat belated—child of the Reformation. Elector John Frederick I the Magnanimous, the head of the Schmalkaldic League, wanted to remove the university library from Wittenberg. Precious prints from the Reformation era are located there, including Luther's personal copies of the Old and New Testaments with handwritten notes by the Reformer, as well as thirty-five volumes of notes by theologian Georg Rörer, one of Luther's students. Next to the university is the City Museum. It displays the "Jenaer Lutherbibel". A memorial to John Frederick I was built in front of the university in 1858. Locals call it the HanFried Memorial (short for Johann Friederich).

THOMAS MÜNTZER, REBEL REFORMER

Initially, Thomas Müntzer was a staunch admirer of Luther and was called to pastorship in Zwickau on the Reformer's recommendation. Müntzer was soon dismissed, however, because of his radical sentiments. He was called to the New City Church (Neustadtkirche) in Allstedt in 1523. Müntzer founded a secret society in 1523, with the goal "of supporting the Gospel, to no longer give any payments to monks and nuns, and to work toward their demise and expulsion."

Luther was greatly troubled by this development. Meanwhile, in a sermon to the princes, Müntzer explained his theological views and demonstrated several areas in which he disagreed with Luther. Müntzer attacked Luther as a conformist hypocrite, while Luther viewed Müntzer as a false prophet, because he explicitly relied on direct revelation from God and downplayed the Bible.

The conflict escalated in the Peasants' War. While Luther viewed peasants who rebelled against and broke the trust of their rulers as murderers and robbers, Müntzer supported such peasants and even instigated a rebellion in Thuringia. Müntzer would not budge from his views and refused to negotiate with Luther. Before the Battle of Frankenhausen, Müntzer wrote to Count Ernst of Mansfeld,

"You wretched, miserable sack of maggots! Who made you the prince of the people?...If you will not humble yourself before the lowly, an eternal disgrace before all Christianity will fall on your neck! You will become the devil's martyr."

Luther was proved right about Müntzer. After the devastating defeat of the peasants in the Battle of Frankenhausen, the rebel leader hid in bed, pretended to be sick, and denied his identity and any association with the Peasants' War. Müntzer was executed in Mühlhausen, Thuringia, on May 27, 1525. A dozen monuments honor him, like this 1957 statue of Müntzer in Mühlhausen.

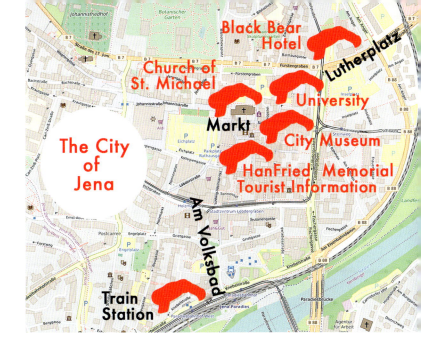

ADDRESSES AND TRAVEL INFORMATION

Tourist Information and Hanfried Memorial
Markt 16, D-07743 Jena
Phone: +49 (0) 3641–49 80 50
www.jenatourismus.de, tourist-info@jena.de

St. Michaelis (Michaeliskirche)
Kirchplatz 1, D-07743 Jena
Phone: +49 (0) 3641–47 16 64 7
www.stadtkirche-jena.de, gemeindebuero.jena@yahoo.de

City Museum (Stadtmuseum)
Markt 7, D- 07743 Jena
Phone: +49 (0) 3641–49 80 38
www.stadtmuseum.jena.de, stadtmuseum@jena.de

Hotel and Restaurant Schwarzer Bär (Black Bear)
Lutherplatz 2, D-07743 Jena
Phone: +49 (0) 3641–40 60
www.schwarzer-baer-jena.de, hotel@schwarzer-baer-jena.de

The Stadtschloss originates from the 10th century, but was often destroyed and rebuilt. It has been a museum since 1923. Among the pieces on display by Lucas Cranach the Elder is the 1522 portrait from Wittenberg, Luther as Junker Jörg.

Weimar's Castle

Weimar is best known for Johann Wolfgang von Goethe. Besides being a famous poet, Goethe was the director of the Duchess Anna Amalia Library for a few decades, founded in 1766. Goethe turned it into one of Germany's finest libraries. It has a one-of-a-kind Bible collection, including a magnificent, richly decorated Luther Bible from 1534. Another treasure is the family register of Pastor Heinrich Kohlhans, bound in light pigskin and featuring the autographs of Martin Luther and Nikolaus von Amsdorf, among others. Luther himself went to the city on the Ilm River quite often. His first trip was documented in 1518, though he was most likely in Weimar earlier as a young monk, as his order maintained a house there.

Weimar was the residence of Elector John the Constant, the brother of Frederick the Wise, After the death of John in 1532, his son John Frederick I, the Magnanimous, took over. But after losing to Charles V in Mühlberg in 1547, he also lost the city of Wittenberg. His wife, Sibylle of Cleves, and the court took refuge in Weimar. Upon his release in 1552, John went to Weimar as well, to live in the City Castle (Stadtschloss). Lucas Cranach the Elder, who had already followed him into exile, joined him in Weimar.

Luther continued to visit John Frederick I; he also preached in the Castle Church known as "Himmelsburg" (Heavenly Palace), numerous times. In 1540, five years before his death, a 57-year-old Luther wrote to his wife, "sweetheart Kate," his last letter from Weimar. He wanted her to "…subserviently know that I am well here. I am eating like a Bohemian and guzzling like a German, thanks be to God, Amen."

Luther had been summoned on this sojourn because his closest Reformation ally and friend, Philipp Melanchthon, was on his deathbed in Weimar. However, a "miracle" occurred, and the gravely ill man became well. The sojourn would be Luther's last of many in the city on the Ilm.

Sights in Weimar

The Sts. Peter and Paul Municipal Church (Herder Church)

Martin Luther occasionally preached in this church. The baptismal font and several chalices date to Luther's time. Epitaphs and gravestones depict rulers from that era. Lucas Cranach the Elder began work on the winged altarpiece in the municipal church, and his son finished it in 1555. The tripartite piece includes a depiction of Martin Luther with an open Bible. Cranach himself is standing beside him, in the stream of blood flowing from Christ.

Former Franciscan Monastery, (Franziskanerkloster)

Only part of this monastic church is left. Luther occasionally preached here. He also spent the night here when visiting Weimar to discuss the Reformation with John Frederick, which is commemorated by a plaque on the building.

Grave of Lucas Cranach the Elder

The Wittenberg painter, who had followed John Frederick I to Weimar in 1552, died in the city one year later. He is buried at Jacobsfriedhof. His gravestone, created by Nikolaus Gromann, was brought to the Herder Church for preservation in 1859. The current stone is a copy, though also made from stone.

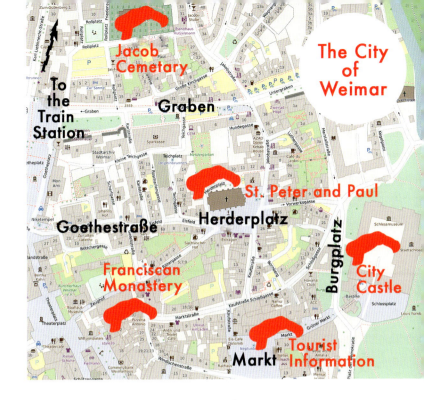

ADDRESSES AND TRAVEL INFORMATION

Tourist Information
Markt 10, D-99423 Weimar
Phone: +49 (0) 3643–74 50
www.weimar.de

St. Peter and Paul Municipal Church (Herder Church)
Herderplatz 8, D-99423 Weimar
Phone: +49 (0) 3643–85 15 18
www.ek-weimar.de, office@ek-weimar.de

City Castle (Stadtschloss)
Burgplatz 4, D-99423 Weimar
www.klassik-stiftung.de/en/start/

Former Franciscan Monastery (Franziskanerkloster)
Am Palais, D-99423 Weimar

Jacob Cemetary (Jakobsfriedhof)
Am Jakobskirchhof, D-99423 Weimar

Model of the Church of St. Paul. Built in 1231, it was consecrated by Luther as a Protestant church in 1544, and torn down by the Communists in 1968. After reunification, this university building was erected.

Chapter Six
Luther's Mission
Spreading the Gospel: Cities of the Reformation

Leipzig, already a prosperous city in the Late Middle Ages, was the seat of the famed Leipzig Disputation between Martin Luther and Johannes Eck, a theology professor from the Bavarian town of Ingolstadt, which took place in June 1519. On Luther's side was Andreas Bodenstein von Karlstadt, his colleague from Wittenberg, before their fallout. On February 7, 1519, Luther wrote to Georg Spalatin: "By the way, our little glory-starved beast, Eck, has published a pamphlet, and according to it, he plans to have a debate with Karlstadt in Leipzig. And since this foolish, jealous man wants to satisfy his long-standing grudge with me, he attacks me and my writings… Consequently, I have published a refutation against him, as you will see." He later added, "It will perhaps give Eck a reason to finally treat this matter seriously, which up to now he has only treated as a game, and to advise the Roman tyranny to their misfortune."

Leipzig, City of Dispute

Many came to hear the "Leipzig Church Battle." Eck, the opponent, was the first to arrive—on June 22, 1519—in order to take part in the Feast of Corpus Christi the following day. The delegation from Wittenberg made its way through the Leipzig gate two days later, also large in number, including Luther, Melanchthon, and Karlstadt. Their arrival was so striking that even Eck was given an honor guard of students from Leipzig. During his stay at Leipzig, Luther and Karlstadt resided in the house of Melchior Lotter, a prominent printer who lived on Hainstrasse, around the corner from the Church of St. Thomas.

After the rules had been negotiated at great length, the debate began on June 27, with a Mass in the Church of St. Thomas, at which the St. Thomas Boys Choir sang. Afterward, the debaters clashed in a battle of words in the Pleissenburg Castle. The debate covered a range of topics including indulgences, the legitimacy of the Pope, free will, and divine grace. While Eck stubbornly defended the didactic authority of the Pope and the supremacy of the Church, Luther took the view that papal infallibility could not be derived from Holy Scripture and that church councils could also err. The debate dragged on for more than seventeen days and ended only because Duke George had invited Elector Joachim of Brandenburg and needed Pleissenburg Castle to accommodate his guests.

Luther and Karlstadt both tried to defeat Eck. In the end, both sides claimed to have won the argument. Nevertheless, Eck regarded himself as the victor and wrote the Pope a letter to that effect in October 1519, asking the Pope to move against Luther for holding to Hussite heresy. Accordingly, a bull threatening excommunication was posted in Meissen, Merseburg, and Brandenburg in September 1520. It applied not only to Luther, but also to Karlstadt and other followers. As a result, Luther's books were burned in several cities. In return, Luther and his followers publicy burned papal books as well the canon law, including the bull threatening excommunication, in Wittenberg. For Luther, the Disputation represented a final break with the Roman Catholic Church. Because of his refusal to recant his Theses on the sale of indulgences, Luther and his followers were finally excommunicated from the church and outlawed by the Emperor in 1521.

Supposedly, Luther went to Leipzig half a year later while holed up in the Wartburg, disguised as "Junker Jörg," on December 3, 1521. He had lunch in a pub at Brühl, a shopping street famous for its furs. A street walker recognized him, however, which upset Luther very much. During a dinner years later, he compared the city to "Sodom and Gomorrra." He also predicted a huge misfortune—though he would not live to see it—in 1547. That was, in fact, the year when Leipzig was besieged by imperial Catholic troops in the Schmalkaldic War. The Pleissenburg, where Luther debated with Eck, was destroyed. The new city hall now in its place is also a very impressive building.

LEIPZIG, CITY OF MUSIC

Leipzig is also famous as the center of Lutheran music, mostly due to Johann Sebastian Bach. The famed cantor of the Church of St. Thomas in Leipzig, who was born in Eisenach in 1658, and had worked previously in Weimar and Köthen, wrote many Lutheran hymns. But Luther also wrote hymns. Toward the end of 1523, Luther shared with Georg Spalatin his plan to write German psalms or spiritual songs for the people, so that the Word of God would remain among the people in song as well. He had already composed "From Depths of Woe I Cry to You" and "May God Bestow on Us His Grace." Now he was looking for additional competent poets, and he turned to Spalatin—among others—for that purpose.

Before writing the hymns mentioned above, Luther had already composed a type of folk song that was circulated as a flyer. It was based on the following incident: In 1523, two of Luther's brother monks were burned to death at the marketplace in Brussels, because of their confession of faith. Even in the first lines, Luther conveys his mood: "We lift up a new song to praise the workings of God our Lord, which God has done for His praise and honor…"

As Otto Schlisske remarked, "Luther is filled with jubilant joy that what he understood to be true had now manifested itself in others as well—and so powerfully that they were even able to bravely face death for it."

> ## Why Hymns were so Important
>
> To appreciate the importance of hymns, we must consider the level of education in Luther's day. Illiteracy was widespread. In the few cities that existed, only about 20 percent of the population was literate. By comparison, in rural areas only an estimated two percent could read and write.
>
> Basically, only clergy and government officials were literate. For this reason, education or instruction could not be imparted by the written word, and religious concepts were conveyed through images in churches. The variety of these images is still visible today.
>
> Back then, the spoken word had even greater significance, and commoners were dependent on "mediators" who could read—especially village priests. For instance, if a priest did not want to read a pamphlet aloud, the information conveyed in it completely bypassed the village. On the other hand, if the priest wanted a text read aloud and wanted to add thoughts of his own that he considered worth sharing, the priest's own ideas would be mixed in with the content of the pamphlet as well.

As early as 1523, Luther's first hymns were published individually. One of them, "Dear Christians, One and All, Rejoice," was one of his most impressive musical compositions. A choral hymnal of four books—one for each voice—contained Luther's first collected musical expressions for singing in worship services. It was published in Wittenberg in 1524.

It was important to Luther that young people in particular learned these songs and enjoyed them. Johann Walter, the cantor of Torgau, is listed as the author of these mostly four-part compositions, while Luther wrote the texts and composed the melodies. In publishing hymnals, he was pursuing various goals. Evangelism was his primary goal, and hymns would spread knowledge of the Bible and the ideas of the Reformation. In addition, rhyming and melody were meant to help people remember Christian content more easily. Finally, singing together would build community. Luther regarded the psychological effects of music as a powerful medicine against evil and as an excellent tool for battling frustration.

Luther composed more than thirty hymns, including hymns for the church year, such as "From Heaven Above to Earth I Come," hymns based on the catechism, such as "These Are the Holy Ten Commandments," hymns based on the Psalms, such as "A Mighty Fortress Is Our God," and liturgical hymns and songs for use at home.

Leipzig, City of Publishing

Shortly after 1500, Leipzig was not only the hub of book printing and publishing in Saxony, but in all of the German-speaking world. The newly developed craft (by Johannes Gutenberg), was of great importance for the progress and stabilization of the Reformation. Luther also knew the power of the printed word and skillfully deployed this new mass medium for his own purposes. Leipzig was where Lutheran texts and numerous evangelical hymn books were printed in large quantities for distribution throughout the country.

Accomplished printing houses such as those of Wolfgang Stöckel, Jacob Thanner, or Melchior Lotter were known far and wide for the quality of their work. They were also among the first to print the Ninety-five Theses in the form of a poster. In 1519, Stöckel also published Luther's speeches from the Leipzig Disputation, with a woodcut depicting the Reformer on the front page. This first picture of him also includes a rose. From then on the rose was known as Luther's emblem, and he used it as his seal beginning in 1530.

The Leipzig printers printed not only Reformation texts, but also increasingly Counter-Reformation posters and books. One reason was Duke George of Saxony's hostile attitude toward the dissemination of Reformation literature. In 1527, he had Nuremberg accountant Hans Hergot executed in Leipzig's market square for publishing the work, On the New Transformation of the Christian Life.

SIGHTS IN LEIPZIG

Church of St. Thomas (Thomaskirche)

St. Thomas, one of two main city churches, dates back to the 12th century; the tower was built in 1537. It is famous for its cantor Johann Sebastian Bach, whose statue stands in front of it. The great composer is know for his many Lutheran hymns, among them *"A Mighty Fortress,"* and the *"Christmas Oratory."* Since 1950, his remains have been in the church (originally he was buried at St. John's Church, destroyed in World War II). Across from St. Thomas is the Bach Museum and Bach Archive. The St. Thomas Boys Choir sings here regularly, including during Sunday services.

Luther introduced the Reformation to Leipzig in this church, at a sermon on Pentecost Sunday, 1539. An 1889 stained-glass window depicts the Leipzig Disputation. On the left is Elector Frederick the Wise, Luther is in the middle, and Philipp Melanchthon is on the right.

Church of St. Nicholas (Nikolaikirche)

This church, completed in 1165, has a Gothic pulpit dating from Luther's time, known for this reason as the Luther Pulpit. Contemporary impressions of the great Reformer can be found at the nearby gallery. In autumn 1989, the Church of St. Nicholas played a crucial role in the Peaceful Revolution, as the site of the Monday peace prayers.

Melchior Lotter's House

Lotter published more than 160 of Luther's texts. He was a friend of the Reformer and sympathised with his ideas. When Luther came to town for the Leipzig Disputation in 1519, he stayed at Lotter's house on Hainstrasse. That same year, Lotter set up a branch of his business in Wittenberg, managed by his sons Melchior and Michael. The original house no longer exists, but a plaque commemorates Lotter.

Auerbach's Keller and Thüringer Hof

Thüringer Hof is the oldest tavern in Leipzig. The cuisine features traditional food from Saxony and Thuringia. Luther often stayed here, as well as at Auerbach's Keller, whose owner, Heinrich Stromer, was a close friend. Luther stayed in his house in 1538.

ADDRESSES AND TRAVEL INFORMATION

Tourist Information
Katharinenstrasse 8, D-04109 Leipzig
Phone: +49 (0) 341–71 04 26 0
www.leipzig.travel, info@ltm-leipzig.de

Church of St. Thomas (Thomaskirche)
Thomaskirchhof 18, D-04109 Leipzig
Phone: +49 (0) 341–22 22 40
www.thomaskirche.org, info@thomaskirche.org

Church of St. Nicholas (Nikolaikirche)
Nikolaikirchhof 3, D-04109 Leipzig
Phone: +49 (0) 341–12 45 38 0
www.nikolaikirche.de, pfarramt@nikolaikirche-leipzig.de

Melchior Lotter's House
Hainstrasse 16-18, D-04109 Leipzig

Auerbach's Keller
Grimmaische Strasse 2-4, D-04109 Leipzig
www.auerbachs-keller-leipzig.de

Thüringer Hof
Burgstrasse 19, D-04109 Leipzig
www.thueringer-hof.de

Hotels in Leipzig

Mariott ****
Am Hallischen Tor 1. D-04109 Leipzig
Phone: +49 (0) 341–9653 0
www.leipzigmarriott.de

Steigenberger Grandhotel Handelshof *****
Salzgässchen 6, D-04109 Leipzig
Phone: +49 (0) 341–350 581 0
leipzig@steigenberger.de,
www.leipzig.steigenberger.com

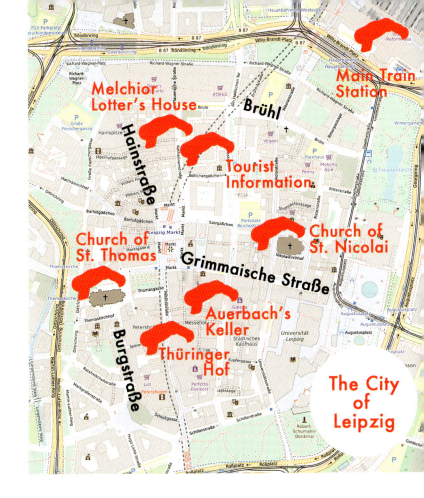

Hotels in Leipzig

Fürstenhof Leipzig *****
Tröndlinring 8, D-04105 Leipzig
Phone: +49 (0) 341–140 0
www.hotelfuerstenhofleipzig.com

Mercure ****
Eutritzscher Strasse 15. D-04105 Leipzig
Phone: +49 (0) 341–30 384 0
h8847@accor.com
www.mercure.com

The Market Church of our Dear Ladies in Halle, with its four towers. It is the home town of George Frideric Handel, standing at Market Square, close to another landmark building, the Red Tower (right).

HÄNDELTOWN HALLE

Halle, with a population of 237,000, is the largest city in Saxony-Anhalt (together with Magdeburg). Located on the Saale River northwest of Leipzig, and connected by commuter train, it is one of the state's oldest cities. Its historic downtown mostly survived World War II. Halle was founded in 806 AD, but it has much older roots. In nearby Nebra, the "Sky Disk" was found, a nearly 4,000-year-old bronze disc with golden ornaments that dates back to the pre-Slavic Únětice culture. It is now at the State Museum of Prehistory.

The most famous son of Halle is Georg Friedrich Händel who was born here in 1685. The composer, whose best-know work is the Messiah, is also known as George Frideric Handel, since he spent most of his career in London. The Händel monument is located in front of the Market Church of Our Dear Ladies, the main church of Halle, where Händel was baptized and his teacher Friedrich Wilhelm Zachow played the organ. In 1702, Händel became the organist at the Church of Our Dear Ladies himself, but left town soon after. Bach's son Wilhelm Friedemann Bach took over as organist. The Missouri Synod of the Lutheran Church in America honors Händel, Bach, and Heinrich Schütz every year on July 28, the day Bach died.

Halle, a member of the Hanse, could stand against clergy and royalty. Surrounded by mines—coal, clay, and salt—the city was rich. Naturally, the House of Wettin that governed Saxony did not like this much. Ernest of Wettin was sent here at age fourteen to become archbishop. To subjugate the citizens, the Wettins built the Moritzburg Castle in 1484. The Moritzburg was mostly destroyed in the Thirty Years' War, but some parts remained. The Wettin royals are buried at the Petersberg monastery outside of Halle.

In 1514, Cardinal Albrecht von Brandenburg, who was also the archbishop of Mainz, took his seat in Halle. Albrecht soon became infamous for his extravagant and sinful lifestyle. He had a number of mistresses and was heavily engaged in selling indulgences to finance them. He also owned churches, castles, and art. He commissioned more than a dozen Cranach pictures alone. The Market Church of Our Dear Ladies was the Cardinal's last big commission, since he needed a prestigious space to store, among other things, 42 holy skeletons. It was also meant to be a bulwark against the Reformation. The church was built between 1529 and 1554, from two medieval churches, St. Gertrude's and St. Mary's, whose naves were demolished, but whose towers—the Blue Towers and the Watchtowers—were retained, making it one of the few four-steepled churches in Germany. It is also the last big and one of the grandest Gothic churches, and has been portrayed by many artists, including Lyonel Feininger.

Albrecht's wasteful behavior outraged many citizens of Halle, and Martin Luther also took a public stand against him. Finally, the city offered to pay his debt to the Fugger banking house. Albrecht left Halle for Mainz in 1541. He took most of his paintings and treasures with him (he stored them in his Aschaffenburg castle, but they were lost in a fire soonafter). On Good Friday that same year, Luther's close friend Justus Jonas held the first Lutheran worship service in Halle, in the Market Church. So Albrecht had unwillingly ushered in the Reformation in his hometown. He died four years later.

Jonas became the first Lutheran bishop of Halle in 1544. Luther came back to Halle twice, in 1545 and 1546, and gave a sermon in the Market Church, commemorated by a 30-foot stone stele. On display inside the church is Luther's death mask and an impression of his hands. When Luther was brought from Eisleben to Wittenberg after his death, his body was laid out in the Halle church for a few days.

Halle's other landmark building is the Red Tower, a watchtower across from the Market Church, built from 1418 to 1506. It was destroyed in World War II, but has been rebuilt since. Halle today is also the main seat of Leucorea, the Martin Luther University founded in Wittenberg.

Sights in Halle

Moritz Castle (Moritzburg)

The Moritzburg, named after patron Saint Maurice, was constructed as a fortified castle in 1484 and partly destroyed in the Thirty Years' War. The Chapel of Mary Magdalene—with the coat of arms of Cardinal Albrecht V of Brandenburg—was restored in 1899, and is considered a Lutheran gem. The castle houses the State Art Museum of Saxony-Anhalt.

The Francke Institution (Franckesche Stiftungen)

The Francke Institutions, founded at Halle in 1698 by theologian and educator August Hermann Francke, house a multitude of cultural, academic, pedagogical, and social facilities. Noteworthy are its coulisse library, the longest half-timbered structure in Europe, and an original museum of art and natural history (Kunst- und Naturalienkammer).

The Halle Cathedral (Dom zu Halle)

The cathedral is the oldest church in old town Halle. Dedicated within a Dominican monastery in 1330, it served as the church of Albrecht von Brandenburg, who had it remodeled in 1523. After he left, the cathedral became Protestant; the exterior was rebuilt again in the Baroque style. The interior houses precious stone figurines, ancient gravestones, and an organ.

Addresses and Travel Information

Tourist Information
Marktplatz 13, D-06108 Halle (Saale)
Phone: +49 (0) 345–12 29 984
www.halle.de/en/Home

Market Church of our Dear Ladies (Marktkirche)
An der Marienkirche 2, D-06108 Halle/Saale
Phone: +49 (0) 345–51 70 894
www.marktkirche-halle.de, marktkirche.halle@web.de

Moritz Castle (Moritzburg)
Friedemann-Bach-Platz 5, D-06108 Halle/Saale
Phone: +49 (0) 345–21 25 90
www.kunstmuseum-moritzburg.de

The Francke Institution (Franckesche Stiftungen)
Franckeplatz 1, Haus 37, D-06110 Halle/Saale
Phone: +49 (0) 345–2 12 74 50
www.francke-halle.de, oeffentlichkeit@francke-halle.de

Cathedral (Dom zu Halle)
Kleine Klausstrasse 6, 06108 Halle (Saale), Germany
Phone: +49 (0) 345–20 21 379
www.ekm-reformiert.de/domgemeinde-halle-startseite/

Sleep in a Thousand Years of History

Today, the Petersburg Monastery is run by the Lutheran Christusbruderschaft (Christ-Brotherhood) Selbitz. It has a very reasonably priced guest house outside of Halle, even cheaper for those willing to do chores.
christusbruderschaft.de/en/direct/index.php

Hotels in Halle (Saale)

TRYP by Wyndham ***
Neustädter Passage 5, D-06122 Halle (Saale)
Phone: +49 (0) 800–1010 880, *www.tryphalle.com*

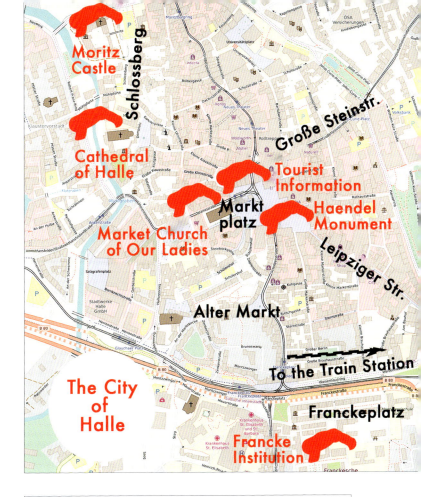

Hotels in Halle (Saale)

Dorint Charlottenhof ****
Dorotheenstrasse 12, D-06108 Halle (Saale)
Phone: +49 (0) 345–29 230, *www.dorint.com*

Dormero Rotes Ross ****
Leipziger Strasse 76, D-06108 Halle (Saale)
Phone: +49 (0) 345–233 430, *www.dormero.de*

Hotel Eigen ***
Kurt-Wüsteneck-Strasse 1, D-06132 Halle (Saale)
Phone: +49 (0) 345–77 556, *www.hotel-eigen.com*

The Naumburg Master created these stone figures. They include the Margraves of Meissen Hermann and Eckard II and their wives Reglindis and Uta. Uta (above) was considered the most beautiful woman in the Middle Ages.

The Naumburg Cathedral

Naumburg is one of the most important Cathedrals of the Middle Ages. Around 1000 AD, Eckard I, Margrave of Meissen, built his new ancestral seat on the Saale River. First known as Nuwenburg, it came to be called Naumburg. In 1028, King Conrad II relocated the Zeitz bishop's see, at the request of Eckard's sons Hermann and Eckard II. Construction of the first Romanesque cathedral began and lasted throughout the next two centuries.

The interior work was done by the Naumburg Master, an anonymous stone sculptor hired by Bishop Dietrich II. The Master designed the cathedral's nave, the west choir, and the rood separating the church lords from the peasants. His crucifixion group near the portal is significant in the history of art. He also crafted the twelve life-size sandstone figures representing territorial lords and patrons laid to rest in the Romanesque building that preceded the current cathedral. Other precious works of art include the oldest stone sculpture of Saint Elizabeth of Thuringia, the altar wings by Lucas Cranach, and the newer windows by Neo Rauch depicting scenes from the life of Saint Elizabeth.

Naumburg's most influential Reformer was Nikolaus Medler, who became superintendent in 1536. He drafted a Luther-approved church- and school ordinance. The last Catholic bishop was Julius von Pflug, appointed in 1540. Protestant Elector John Frederick, however, appointed Nikolaus von Amsdorf as the city's first Lutheran bishop, a confidant and unwavering ally of Luther. When the Protestants were defeated in the Schmalkaldic War, Amsdorf was forced to flee, and Pflug assumed the office of bishop. However, because nearly all of his flock had become Protestant, Pflug sought a conciliatory path. Since 1939, a figurative representation of Luther on the pulpit in the cathedral commemorates that act.

The cathedral is at Domplatz 16–17, D-06618 Naumburg. More at *www.naumburg-cathedral.de/*

The Frauenkirche, built in 1726, destroyed in 1945, and rebuilt in 2005. A statue of Luther stands here, created by Adolf von Dönnhof in 1885 and cast in bronze at the local bell foundry. Since World War II, it has been restored.

Our Lady of Dresden

The Church of Our Lady in Dresden, the Frauenkirche, is an internationally renowned example of Lutheran architecture that attracts tens of thousands of tourists every year. Dresden, the capital of Saxony with a population of half a million, is located on the Elbe River. Initially the Reformation attracted very few supporters there, however. Luther visited Dresden in 1516 and 1518, just one year after nailing his Thesis to the Castle Church. He was sent by his order of the Augustinian Monastery. He received a warm welcome from Duke George the Bearded, but little sympathy for his ideas.

George was a cousin of Frederick the Wise. He belonged to the Albertine branch of the Wettins, who sided with Charles V in the Schmalkaldic War. In 1523, he even had every Lutheran Bible confiscated. Luther's followers, however, subsequently did take the Reformation to Dresden. The Frauenkirche was built from 1726–1743, followed by the Martin Luther Church in Dresden-Neustadt in 1883–1887.

The Frauenkirche dates back to the 11th century, when the first church dedicated to Our Lady was built. It became protestant after the Reformation. Lutheran hymnist Heinrich Schütz, who is regarded as the forerunner of Bach, was buried in this church after he died in Dresden in 1672. His grave was destroyed, however, when the church was torn down in 1727. It was replaced by the much larger Baroque Lutheran parish church (albeit not the seat of a bishop), paid for by the citizens of Dresden. Even though Saxon Elector Frederick August I reconverted to Roman Catholicism to become King of Poland and Lithuania in 1697, he supported the construction, since it added one of the largest cupolas in Europe to his residence, which has been painted many times.

Famous organ maker Gottfried Silberman constructed a three-manual instrument for the church, with 43 stops. The organ was dedicated on November 25, 1726. Johann Sebastian Bach gave a recital there on December 1.

The Frauenkirche was destroyed in the Allied bombing of Dresden during the final weeks of World War II, on February 13, 1945. Firebombs killed about 50,000 people, including many refugees from the East. The church itself was targeted for two days and one night, until the pillars finally collapsed, burying the altar and the organ. A few hundred Dresdeners who had sought refuge there managed to get out. Martin Luther's own handwritten copy of his first lecture as professor of theology at Wittenberg ("*Commentarios* in psalmos Davidis, 1513–1516"), had been safeguarded in a vault there, along with the score of Bach's Mass in B minor, and is now in Saxony's state library.

East German leaders ordered the blackened piles of stones and rubble to be left as a memorial to World War II. Only after reunification was the church rebuilt. The citizens of Dresden collected donations. An American initiative was led by Günter Blobel, a German-born American, who survived World War II near Dresden. When he won the Nobel Prize for medicine, he donated all of the award money, nearly $1 million, to the restoration of Dresden. Reconstruction took twelve years, with the help of old pictures and memories. Some thousand stones and original altar parts were reused, still visible within the building due to their darker color. The organ, however, has not been rebuilt.

Addresses and Travel Information

Get there by car: Autobahn A 4 from Köln and Eisenach to Poland passes Dresden. A 13 connects Berlin with Dresden;

Get there by train: The IC from Berlin as well as the ICE from Leipzig stops at the Dresden main station. Dresden is also connected to Vienna, Budapest, Bratislava and Prague. However, most of the tracks are not high-speed. so the trains are somewhat slower than usual. Buses are a good alternative.

Tourist Information
Münzgasse 2, D-01067 Dresden
Phone: +49 (0) 351–65 31 88 82
www.touristeninformation-dresden.de
info@touristeninformation-dresden.de

Church of Our Lady (Frauenkirche)
Neumarkt, D- 01067 Dresden
Phone: +49 (0) 351–65 60 61 00
www.frauenkirche-dresden.de
stiftung@frauenkirche-dresden.de

Hotels in Dresden

Best Western Dresden ****
Buchenstrasse 10, D-01097 Dresden
Phone: +49 (0) 351–81 51 50 0
www.best-western-dresden.de

Hotel Taschenbergpalais Kempinski *****
Taschenberg 3, D-01067 Dresden
Phone: +49 (0) 351–49 12 0
www.kempinski.com/en/dresden/hotel-taschenbergpalais

Steigenberger Hotel de Sax *****
Neumarkt 9, D-01067 Dresden
Phone: +49 (0) 351–43 86 0
www.steigenberger.de

Castle Hartenfels in Torgau, the seat of the Ernestines. From here, Frederick the Wise protected the Reformation. Today, the Castle is a museum, devoted to the rich history of the area, and a place for festivals and concerts.

Torgau at the Elbe

Torgau is mostly known today because it is where the American and the Soviets soldiers met in World War II. The picture of their historic handshake was printed all over the world, and is also displayed at the Torgau train station. A memorial to the event stands at the Elbe River. But Torgau's heyday was in the first half of the 16th century, when it was one of the most important and earliest cities in which the Reformation took place. The reason for both was its proximity to Wittenberg, but also because Frederick the Wise and the Ernestine branch of the Saxon Electors established their residence in Torgau. They remodeled Hartenfels Castle (Schloss Hartenfels), with its round "Hausmannsturm" (Watchman's Tower), into a place to live. Hartenfels is the largest German castle of the early Renaissance period.

Torgau caught on to the Reformation early. In 1519, the first German-language baptism took place in the Church of St. Nicholas. The church was secularized soon after and is now part of the inner courtyard of Torgau's city hall. In 1520, the first Protestant sermon was held in German, and Luther preached in Torgau in 1522. One year later, the City Council closed every cloister in its vicinity. Statues of saints and paintings in churches were destroyed, in the spirit of the followers of Andreas Bodenstein von Karlstadt. Citizens stormed the Franciscan monastery. This was too much for Luther; after Karlstadt was exiled from Saxony, he forced his followers to leave Torgau in 1529.

John Frederick I, the Magnanimous, who followed Frederick the Wise, turned Torgau into a center of politics and also the political center of the Reformation. He formed the League of Torgau, an alliance of Protestant rulers. In March 1530, Luther, together with Melanchthon and Bugenhagen, developed the Torgau Articles, the theological guidelines for the Diet of Augsburg as well as for the Augsburg Confession. In 1544, Luther consecrated Torgau's Castle Church in the side wing, the first Protestant church in Torgau. Luther regularly preached in the castle chapel. Only recently has the chapel been renovated and reopened. All in all, the Reformer traveled to Torgau more than forty times.

Torgau is the final resting place of Katharina von Bora, Luther's wife. Sadly, when Luther died in 1546, her life became a struggle. As if economic hardship were not bad enough, she had to flee to Magdeburg to avoid being caught up in the Schmalkaldic War, and later to Braunschweig.

She returned to Wittenberg, but the Black Abbey was destroyed in the war. Torgau had been the first place where the then-twenty-four-year old nun had gone after she escaped the convent. In 1552, she sought shelter in Torgau again, mostly to escape the plague. On that journey, she had an accident, broke her hip, and never recovered. Katharina von Bora died on December 20, 1552, at age fifty-three, six years after the death of her husband and shortly after the eighteenth birthday of her youngest daughter Margarethe. She was honored with a burial in the City Church of St. Mary.

Shortly before his death, on January 25, 1546, Luther wrote his wife, Katharina:

"To my kind, dear Katie… Today at eight we left Halle but could not reach Eisleben. Instead, we got back to Halle at nine, because the 'Anabaptist' floods of the river confronted us with waves of water and huge ice floes. Inundating the whole countryside, the waters threatened to 'rebaptize' us. Yet we were also unable to return because of the Mulde River near Bitterfeld, and we remained captive here at Halle, surrounded by water—not that we are thirsting to drink it, since we have good beer from Torgau and good Rhine wine. Meanwhile, we are refreshing and consoling ourselves with those beverages, in the hope that the Saale River will subside. Because even the locals and ferrymen were fainthearted, we did not want to cross the water and tempt God. For the devil is ill-intentioned toward us and lives in the water."

SIGHTS IN TORGAU

Church of St. Mary (Marienkirche)

St. Mary's dates back to a Romanesque church, but most parts were built in the 14th century. It has three naves and two steeples, one of which has a Baroque spire. The pulpit is adorned by a clock. A number of tombs are within its walls, namely Sophie von Mecklenburg's tomb, the first wife of John the Steadfast, and the tomb of Katharina von Bora.

House of Katharina von Bora (Katharina-Luther Stube)

The house at Katharinenstrasse, where Luther's wife died, is now a memorial and a small museum with a permanent exhibit about everyday life in the Luther household and Katharina's biography. Visitors can even pose as the Luthers (photo left). This is not the only place in Torgau devoted to Luther's widow. The "Herr Käthe" Restaurant (Mr. Käthe), which is what Luther called his strict and determined wife, is within the premises of Hartenfels Castle, with a view of St. Mary's.

Old Superintenditure (Alte Superintendentur)

This building near Hartenfels Castle is where Luther and his fellow theologians met to draft the Torgau Articles in 1530. The edifice was renovated only recently.

Spalatin House (Spalatinhaus)

This house on Katharinenstrasse is where Georg Spalatin resided, the intermediary between Luther and the Wettin Electors who resided in Castle Hartenfeld. During Luther's era, many impressive homes were built for the upper classes. They had rooms with arched ceilings and splendid frescos, some of which have been preserved. The Spalatin House is currently being renovated.

Hotels in Torgau:

Central Hotel ***
Friedrichplatz 8, D-04860 Torgau
Phone: +49 (0) 3421–73 28 0
www.central-hotel-torgau.alsterweb.de/

Torgauer Brauhof Hotel und Restaurant ***

Warschauer Strasse 7, D-04860 Torgau
Phone: +49 (0) 3421–73 00 15
www.torgauer-brauhof.de
info@torgauer-brauhof.de

Hotel Goldener Anker

Markt 6, D-04860 Torgau
Phone: +49 (0) 3421–73 21 3
www.goldener-anker-torgau.de

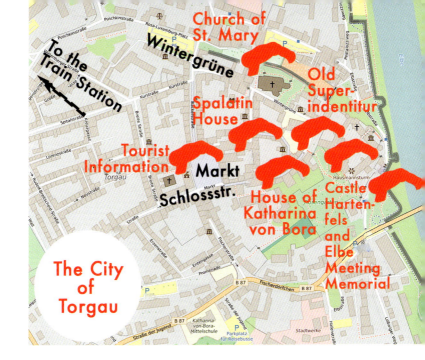

ADDRESSES AND TRAVEL INFORMATION

Tourist Information
Markt 1, D-04860 Torgau
Phone: +49 (0) 3421–70 14 0
www.tic-torgau.de, info@tic-torgau.de

Katharina von Bora-House (Katharina-Luther Stube)
Katharinenstrasse 11, D-04860 Torgau

Spalatin House (Spalatinhaus)
Katharinenstrasse 8, D-04860 Torgau

Castle Hartenfels (Schloss Hartenfels)
Schlossstr. 27, D-04860 Torgau
www.schloss-hartenfels.de, info@schloss-hartenfels.de

Church of St. Marien (Marienkirche)
Wintergrüne 2, D-04860 Torgau
www.evkirchetorgau.de, evkirchetorgau@t-online.de

Old Superindentitur (Alte Superintendentur)
Schlossstrasse 27, D-04860 Torgau

LUTHER IN WORMS

The most important testimony to Protestant history in Worms is the Luther Memorial, the largest Reformation Memorial in the world, designed and constructed by Ernst Rietschel and his scholars. In the center is Martin Luther with his Bible, surrounded by other Reformers, such as John Wycliffe, Peter Waldo, Girolamo Savonarola, and Jan Hus, along with supporters like Frederick the Wise of Saxony, Philipp Landgrave of Hesse, Johannes Reuchlin, and Philipp Melanchthon. The steles and medallions refer to different Reformation sites. The three ladies symbolize the three cities Speyer, Augsburg, and Magdeburg, important for the Reformation.

The Worms City Museum in St. Andrew's Collegiate Church has a Luther Room featuring a Luther Bible, and the Trinity Church on the Market Square shows Luther's appearance at the Imperial Diet in a mosaic on a tower wall. Five stained-glass windows illustrate the creed and Luther's declarations. The Worms tourist office offers a guided tour in costume, especially for groups.

Find further information at *www.worms.de.*

The Reformation in Speyer

The tallest steeple in the Palatinate dominates the cityscape of Speyer. At just under a thousand feet, it soars above all of the other buildings in the city, even the cathedral. It belongs to the Gedächtniskirche, the Memorial Church built between 1893 and 1904, in the Neo-Gothic style.

Its construction was supposed to be a reminder of the protest action that the imperial evangelical states brought to bear at the Reichstag in Speyer in 1529. On April 19, 1529, six princes and 14 imperial free cities representing the Protestant minority in the Holy Roman Empire petitioned the Imperial Diet at Speyer against the Imperial Ban against Martin Luther, and against the proscription of his works and teachings. They called for the unhindered spread of the "evangelical" faith. This was the birth of the word "Protestant." The Luther memorial in the vestibule and the adjacent statues of local Protestant rulers serve as reminders of this event.

On October 31, 2017, the main Reformation service in Rheinland Palatinate will take place at the Memorial Church in Speyer.

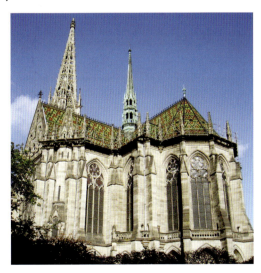

Selected Literature and Sources

Bainton, Roland H. *Martin Luther.* Translated by Hermann Dorries. 3d ed. Göttingen, 1959. Title of the original English edition: *Here I Stand: A Life of Martin Luther.*

Brecht, Martin. *Martin Luther.* 3 vols. Stuttgart, 1986 (Brecht).

Bretschneider, Carolus Gottlieb, ed. *Corpus Reformatorum* (CR). Vol. 11. Halle, 1843.

Beutel, Albrecht. *Luther Handbuch.* Tübingen, 2005.

Hürlimann, Martin, ed. *Martin Luther dargestellt von seinen Freunden und Zeitgenossen etc.* Berlin, 1933 (Hürlimann).

Junghans, Helmer. *Martin Luther und Wittenberg.* Munich, 1996.

Kostlin, Julius. *Martin Luther: Sein Leben und seine Schriften.* Vols. 1–2. 2nd ed. Eberfeld, 1883 (Köstlin).

Lilje, Hans. Luther. Reinbeck bei Hamburg, 1965. 17th ed., 1994.

Luther, Martin. *D. Martin Luthers Werke: Kritische Gesamtausgabe* (WA). 73 vols. in 85. Weimar: H. Bohlau, 1883.

— *D. Martin Luthers Werke: Briefwechsel* (WA Br). 18 vols. Weimar: H. Bohlau, 1930.

— *D. Martin Luthers Werke: Deutsche Bibel* (WA DB). 12 vols. in 15. Weimar: H. Bohlau, 1906.

— *D. Martin Luthers Werke: Tischreden* (WA TR). 6 vols. Weimar: H. Bohlau, 1912–21.

— *Dr. Martin Luthers sämmtliche Schriften: Neue revidirte Stereotypausgabe* (StL). 23 vols. in 25. St. Louis: Concordia, 1880–1910.

— *Die gantze Heilige Schrifft Deudsch 1545.* Edited by Hans Volz and Heinz Blanke. Reprinted in 2 vols. (Volz).

Matthesius, M. Johann. *D. Martin Luthers Leben in siebzehn Predigten.* Edited by Georg Buchwald. Leipzig, 1887 (Matthesius).

Mechthild von Magdeburg. *Das fließende Licht der Gottheit. Eine Auswahl.* Edited by Gisela Vollmann-Profe. Stuttgart: Reclam, 2008.

Oberman, Heiko. *Luther, Mensch zwischen Gott und Teufel.* Berlin, 1982.

Schlisske, Otto. *Handbuch der Lutherlieder.* Gottingen, 1948.

Steinwachs, Albrecht, and Jürgen Pietsch. *Die Stadtkirche der Lutherstadt Wittenberg.* Wittenberg, 2000.

Treu, Martin. *Luther und Torgau.* Wittenberg, 1995.

— *Katharina von Bora.* Wittenberg, 1995.

Warnke, Martin. *Cranachs Luther.* Frankfurt am Main, 1984.

Picture Credits

Bundesarchiv, Bild 183-60015-0002 / Giso Löwe / CC-BY-SA 3.0: p. 162.
CEphoto, Uwe Aranas / CC-BY-SA-3.0: p. 104 above, p. 130 below.
CMR/Christiane Würtenberger: pp. 102, 128, 134, Jessica Mintelowsky: p. 131 above.
Grigoleit, Bert: p. 160.
Investitions- und Marketinggesellschaft Sachsen-Anhalt mbH: p. 9 (Jens Wolf), p. 38 (Michael Bader), p. 45 below (Jörg Gläscher), p. 61, p. 68 (Hagen Neßler), p. 70 (Jörg Gläscher), p. 75 below (Klaus-Peter Voigt), p. 104.
Public Domain: pp. 18, 21, 52, 53, 54, 55, 56, 57, 58, 59, 60, 88.
Pummpälzweg e.V. : p. 98 below.
Schweitzer, Eva C.: pp. 22, 28, 33, 36, 39, 40, 41, 42, 43, 44, 45 above, 48, 49, 50, 69, 74, 75 above, 76, 82 above, below, 83, 108, 112, 113, 114 middle, below, 123, 124, 125, 126 above, below, 142, 148 above, 149 above, middle, 164, 167, 168 middle.
Stadtverwaltung Mansfeld: pp. 64, 67 above, middle, below.
Thüringer Tourismus GmbH: p. 98 above (Andreas Weise), p. 99 above, below (Andreas Weise), p. 118 (Paul Hentschel), p. 131 below.
Tourismus-Region Anhalt-Dessau-Wittenberg e.V.: p. 67 above, 67. below.
Wartburg Stiftung Eisenach: p. 92.
Weimar GmbH: p. 138 (Klapproth und Koch), p. 140 above (Maik Schuck).
Wikimedia: p. 76 above (Erwin Meier), p. 78 (Prinz Wilbert), p. 81 (Chris 73), p. 86 (Doris Antony), p. 89 (Thomas Gatz), p. 90 (David Meisel), p. 91 (Doris Antony), p. 104 below (Robert Scarth), p. 105 (Selby), p. 114 above (GFreihalter), p. 115 above (Wikswat), p. 115 middle (Jan Hauke), p. 115 below (Z Thomas), p. 126 middle (CTHOE), p. 130 above (Tommes-Wiki), p. 135 (Felix Q), p. 136 (Michael Schmalenstroer), p. 140 middle (Most Curious), p. 140 below (Michael VE), p. 148 below (Martin Geisler), p. 149 below (Martin Geisler), p. 152 (Omits), p. 155 above (M*tth.K), p. 155 middle (M_H.DE), p. 155 below (Dbachmann), p. 158 (Fewskulchor), p. 168 above (Jungpionier), p. 170 (User ID), p. 171 (Immanuel Giel).

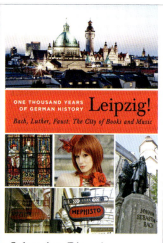

Sebastian Ringel
LEIPZIG!
One Thousand Years of German History
Softcover, 224 pp., $24.95
ISBN: 978-1-935902-58-1

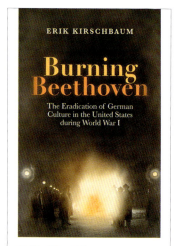

Erik Kirschbaum
BURNING BEETHOVEN
The Eradication of German Culture during World War I
Softcover, 176 pp., $13.95
ISBN: 978-1-935902-85-0

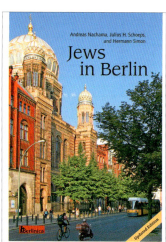

Andreas Nachama
Julius Schoeps
Hermann Simon
JEWS IN BERLIN

Softcover, 310 pp., $24,95
ISBN: 978-1-935902-60-7

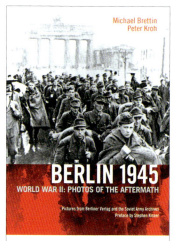

Michael Brettin
BERLIN 1945
Photos of the Aftermath
Softcover, 218 pp., $23.95
ISBN: 978-1-935902-02-7
Preface by Steven Kinzer

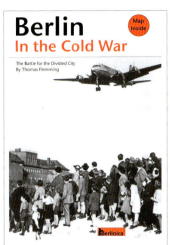

Thomas Flemming
BERLIN IN THE COLD WAR
Softcover, 96 pp., $10.95
ISBN: 978-1-935902-80-5
With a map of Cold War places

Erik Kirschbaum
ROCKING THE WALL
The Berlin Concert that Changed the World
Softcover, 176 pp., $17.95
ISBN: 978-1-935902-82-9

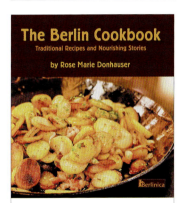

Rose Marie Donhauser
THE BERLIN COOKBOOK
Traditional Recipes and Nourishing Stories

Softcover, 104 pp., $16.95
ISBN: 978-1-935902-50-8

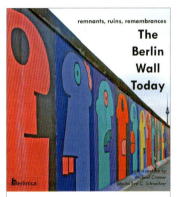

Michael Cramer
THE BERLIN WALL TODAY
Remnants, Ruins Remembrances

Softcover, 86 pp., $14.95
Full Color
ISBN: 978-1-935902-10-2

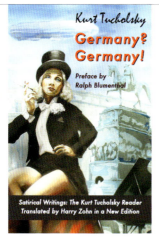

Kurt Tucholsky
GERMANY? GERMANY!
Satirical Writings
Translated by Harry Zohn
Softcover, 200pp., $14.95
ISBN: 978-1-935902-38-6

Kurt Tucholsky
BERLIN! BERLIN!
Dispatches from the
Weimar Republic
Softcover, 198 pp., $13.95
ISBN: 978-1-935902-23-3

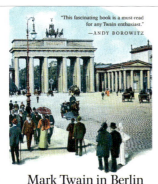

Andreas Austilat
MARK TWAIN IN BERLIN
Newly Discovered Stories
Softcover, 176 pp., $14.95
ISBN: 978-1-935902-95-9
Preface by Lewis Lapham

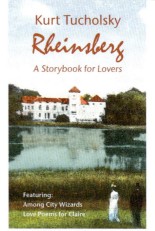

Kurt Tucholsky
RHEINSBERG
A Storybook for Lovers
Hardcover, 96 pp., $14.95
ISBN: 978-1-935902-25-6